The Way

A Celtic Qabalah

JOHN HUNT PUBLISHING

First published by O-Books, 2008
O-Books is an imprint of John Hunt Publishing Ltd., 3 East St., Alresford,
Hampshire SO24 9EE, UK
office@jhpbooks.com
www.johnhuntpublishing.com
www.o-books.com

For distributor details and how to order please visit the 'Ordering' section on our website.

ISBN: 978 1 84694 136 8
978 1 78535 577 6 (ebook)

A CIP catalogue record for this book is available from the British Library.

Design: Stuart Davies

UK: Printed and bound by CPI Group (UK) Ltd, Croydon, CR0 4YY
US: Printed and bound by Thomson-Shore, 7300 West Joy Road, Dexter, MI 48130

The Way

A Celtic Qabalah

Rev John Littlewood

BOOKS

Winchester, UK
Washington, USA

Contents

i. Preface

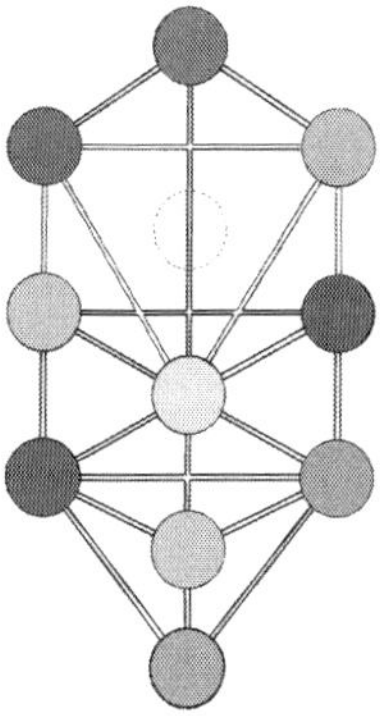

The way I see it, the Qabalah can be understood as a diagram of the mind with various offered routes to explore. Following these routes give a deeper understanding of that mind. It is a most profound diagram or symbol that came into prominence during the third century of the Christian era, although it developed within the Jewish mystical tradition. At that time it was meant to be used as a means of transcending the finite limitations of mortal man to approach an inner acceptance and knowing of the infinite greatness of God. But such a symbol and system couldn't possibly remain exclusive for long, so subsequently it was hijacked by the Gnostics to help explain the nature of creation, then by the western magical tradition as a means to gain power over self and others, and then again by cults and individuals within the New Age spirituality as a means to become godlike, to grow in spirit or "enter a new dimension of being"!

My approach has been to look at the different interpretations and reinterpretations over the centuries, to delve beneath the presented symbols that are held in these various frameworks and to try to understand the basic principles of the Qabalah itself. That seems a tall order, but from that groundwork I have tried to build up a new set of images that is not dependent upon the past or borrowed from any religious setting other than from these Isles.

This book is essentially a workbook. It presents a system to develop self-awareness, to provide a therapeutic framework, to be seen as a mystical and magical pathway and a widening of understanding of all things spiritual and religious. It is not an idle read. You really have to work on the exercises in order to keep up, for this is not a parlor game. It is serious stuff.

These exercises are not just a point of interest, just something to read and think about. They are, in effect, a discipline to follow – a regular meditative exercise to practice. If they remain just an intellectual point of discussion then I have failed in some way. In that case it is like a very special meal that has taken hours to prepare but where the people who sit down at the meal table just look at the plate and intellectualize over the type of food. A discussion may follow about its nutritional value or the colors and layout of presentation. But the people remain hungry and empty because they do not even attempt to eat anything for it may spoil the presentation or be too much like hard work when chewing if they do!

I have found it best if a regular pattern is adopted that fits into the general working day without too much upheaval. In other words, find a slot that slips into the daily routine without too much hassle. Then the new routine will most likely become the regular daily cycle and any lapse will feel odd! At least try for two or three slots each week for the visualizations to be most effective, using whichever exercise you feel you need to develop for each occasion, rather than simply doing each one in turn. Try it and see. There is no alternative to experience – however, do take great care for the mind has extraordinary abilities and potentials. The exercising of it in this manner may have unexpected results.

Therefore this is a version of the Qabalah more in keeping with western Celtic imagery. It is an endeavor to rid the Qabalah path workings of the religious jargon and gobbledygook that abounds around the subject. All that kind of thing is likely to confuse, get in the way, or generally obfuscate rather than enable development and serious investigation. I sometimes wonder if all the high religious words and imagery contained in most books on the subject are more to boost the ego or self-acclamation of the writer rather than assist the reader or novice worker.

I hope not to fall into the same trap but to open up the fascinating world of the Qabalah in a way that intrigues the reader and encourages him or her to investigate its potential.

Rev John Littlewood

1. Principles of Approach

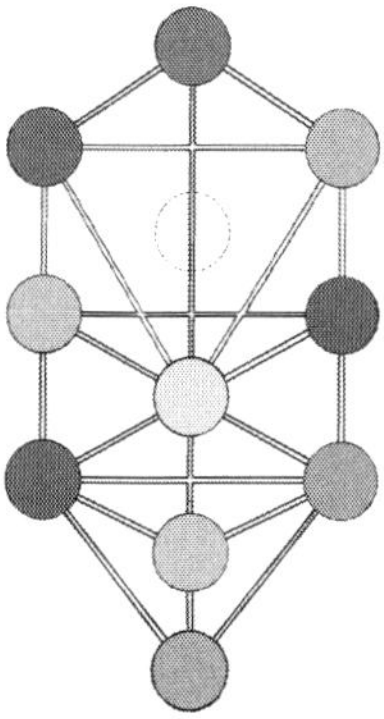

Looking back to the time of the English Reformation, the sight that presented itself to Archbishop Thomas Cranmer was a church worship that was totally irrelevant to the time and the people. It was riddled with superstition - or at best religious mysticism - often spoken in Latin and based on the seven services of the monastic day. That might have been fine for the monks enclosed in their own special world but for the average man-in-the-street it was nonsense. Cranmer's reforming zeal was to put in place a form of worship that would last for the next 300 years, enabling anyone to understand what was going on and to worship in a meaningful way. That is the kind of example I tried to follow in the reworking of the Qabalah.

Far too often when picking up a book or explanation of the Qabalah you find yourself struggling with a plethora of religious sounding words and jargon that immediately puts you off looking any deeper. The Qabalah is complicated enough in its own right without additional details, but usually the reworked example that greets the reader tends to begin with a Jewish word or symbol and then proceeds to make use of all manner of other symbols, borrowing from any and all religions, past and present alike. This may show that the origins of this system of thought are placed clearly in the Jewish Mystical Tradition, but it does not really help much unless those symbols hold some meaning and power for you. The words and symbols have no power in themselves; they remain only shapes on the paper or sounds in the air. They only gain power and meaning in the minds and wills of the people who use them. It might as well be written in Archaic Old English, Latin or Greek and use the symbols that the people who spoke such languages would have been familiar with, for all the good it does. Most of us are not Old Hebrew, Old English, Old Roman or Greek.

Furthermore, today the usual mix of contexts tends to rely heavily upon the Tarot, Ancient Egyptian and Greek mythology, Biblical symbolism and American Shamanistic traditions. The writers tend to rely upon the reader having some degree of understanding of these frameworks, varying upon the reason and use of each tradition. Many people would argue that it is not necessary to understand the symbols being used, but only to get on and use them! On the whole I agree, but I will write further about this when explaining something of the mechanism of visualization. At the moment, suffice it to say, let me simply state that some symbols work better than others, and these not necessarily always being the same for each and every person in identical situations. We are different from each other and would expect the strengths of reaction or effectiveness to differ from person to person depending upon that person's background, their individual spiritual path, their expectations in life and their mental and emotional makeup.

All that surely sounds like serious and heavy work right from the start, so leaving aside the mechanics of 'path working' or visualizations for the moment, lets just acknowledge that any translation loses some of the subtlety and meaning of the piece no matter how carefully that translation is done. To burden the reader with the extra hurdle of transposition [if not actual translation] from one context to another, is to my mind, one burden that is uncalled for. I am a westerner of Caucasian extraction and my ancestors are a mix of Celt, Norseman, Mediterranean and Middle-European. I am British, and I wish I could have found an exposition of the Qabalah more in the Celtic tradition for myself years ago. Then at least my rational mind might have begun to understand more fully the concepts and the depth of investigation that could have opened before me, and my emotional anguish be assuaged.

Unfortunately, the Celtic language was more spoken than written, so despite the Celtic Ogham script or runes, much richness of legend and tradition was lost in the mists of time. The sagas of the North mean very little to me and have even less of an attraction for me to find out more. The Mediterranean myths and legends are sometimes told in film or book so those tales may ring bells for me, but I get lost in all the names and relationships between the gods and heroes and their respective deeds for good or ill. I prefer to leave them all well alone and consign them along with the Egyptian pantheon of gods and goddesses to academic curiosity and theological debate. I do not want to become a disciple in those traditions, no matter how slight my following might be, although they do remain a point of interest.

There is still resonance with the things of nature though, for nature has its own language and means of speaking that the ages have hardly changed. The weather, the lie of the land, animals, birds, trees, rocks and water all have a power to encapsulate symbolic meaning. It therefore remains mainly with these that the visualization exercises are constructed. I must, however, own up to my own mix of theological bits and pieces that have crept in alongside nature. Even if I keep to the artifacts that remain of standing stones, circles, barrows and wells, I must point out that these do belong to the Old Religion. So I cannot totally stand aside from my own criticism of non-understanding or of placing images within a religious context. Yet these *are* a part of my deep heritage and cultural psyche and, try as I might, they unexpectedly appear along with monks or cowled figures, castles and dragons. I tried to minimize their appearances and endeavored to remain true to ethnic and universal symbolism, so I therefore beg forgiveness for arbitrariness in the use of them all from the outset.

The last section of each exercise is where I try to compare the given visualization exercise with other established frameworks. To be as true to the principles already spoken of I will, of necessity, keep each of these sections as short as possible. My intention is just to show that the correspondence does apply and not to amplify this in any way.

There is one exception, in that the Tarot card normally associated with a particular position in the Qabalah is normally due to its order of presentation in the pack. I have deliberately *not* accepted this positioning as if it was 'gospel', but rather looked for a card within that system that is more applicable to the descriptive principles of each position. I am not inventing or claiming another layout - I am definitely flying in the face of convention - I am only looking within the images of the Tarot pack for, in my logic, a more apt correspondence.

2. The Tree of Life - the Journey of the Soul

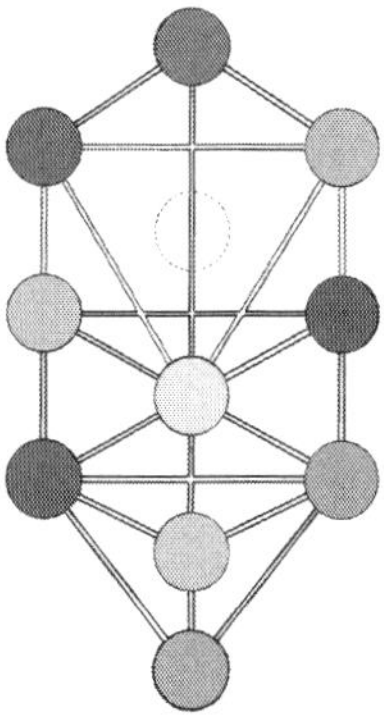

If someone ever gets to enjoy the luxury of respite from the endless struggle to survive, then an urge that crops up from time to time is the need to understand the world better - to take time out to understand the relationship between self and others or to understand the relationship between self, others and the rest of Creation. That might sound rather academic or intellectual but in fact it truly isn't. It is a preoccupation that is at the root of the nation's voyeuristic tendencies, to vicariously experience drama through the TV 'soaps' or 'Big Brother'. Call it just curiosity, the thirst for knowledge or downright snooping. It depends upon the level of enquiry and the integrity of the enquirer as to which is the best description, but even at its most basic the individual is sifting knowledge and comparing that with past experience and present anticipation. It is when the quest is formalized that it becomes the prerogative of religion, psychology or marriage guidance and the like and then, altruistically or euphemistically, it is entitled "The Journey of the Soul".

The Qabalah can be used within that quest. As I said before, it is a system or framework that has been used for different purposes at different periods of history and in different countries of the world. Despite that it has been depicted throughout by the same symbol, instantly recognized with its circles and lines, but the interpretation and area of quest has ranged from the nature of God, the nature of Creation, to the nature of Magic and the nature of Mankind.

It is a profound thought that the same symbol can be used for so different an investigation or even all investigations at the same time. Unfortunately, that has contributed to the complexity and mystery that surrounds it and lends it to misuse by the egotist to show his or her erudition. Perhaps the greatest tragedy of all is that the complexity has deterred the 'ordinary person' of its use, for provided the principles have been grasped, its sheer profundity leaves a bottomless depth to plunge into, again and again, never exhausting the further possibility of self knowledge and growth. *That* is the Journey of the Soul, the inward looking or soul-searching that gives rise to spirituality, respect and maturity.

Of course there are dangers on that route. Of course it is helpful if those conversant with the system can share their experiences to guide others following on, but it still remains a *solitary* journey that each one of us makes to some degree or other – no matter if we pretend to journey with like-minded people, belonging to a Church or group or corporate identity. Essentially we journey alone.

Evolving over the years, and although trying to shed light on deep mysteries, the slightly different frameworks themselves ironically provide further layers of mystery and interpretation to the casual investigator. If the individual eventually works through that and finds the system a means of discovery, then it has achieved its basic function - enabling, encouraging and empowering. For the most part, however, the associated religious symbols explaining that central symbol of the Tree of Life surround it with layer after layer, *obscuring* truth and insight. Each Qabalah framework has its time and place, but once that time has passed the religious remnants can only trip or confuse. So courage is needed for each generation of enquirer to think afresh and present the truth in ways that reveal and lead on. As we delve within, I trust that can be said of this presentation.

i. The Languages of the Mind

The Qabalah is just one diagram of the inner person, the mind. There are many others, all equally valid, even though they might not each convey the same degree or profundity of meaning. Each one offers a different perspective or way of looking at the mind that helps us form a better understanding. Let me first write of two others.

1. The Lower Unconscious
2. The Middle Unconscious
3. The Higher Unconscious or Superconscious
4. The Field of Consciousness
5. The Conscious Self or 'I'
6. The Higher Self
7. The Collective Unconscious

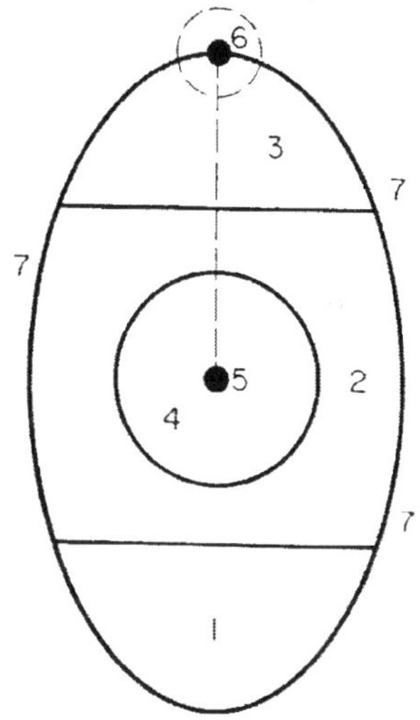

Assagioli - an Italian doctor and psychologist - described the inner person like an egg. The innermost point is the conscious mind and the expanding layers, being less and less dense, represent the subconscious, which gradually merges with others to form the group consciousness. His main point is that the conscious mind is so small and insignificant with regard to the subconscious. It can also be considered that each person is an island of consciousness in a sea of mind, and it is extremely difficult to ascertain the boundaries between the different layers of being.

Jung's diagram is an inversion of this, yet again showing the comparative significance of the conscious mind as against the

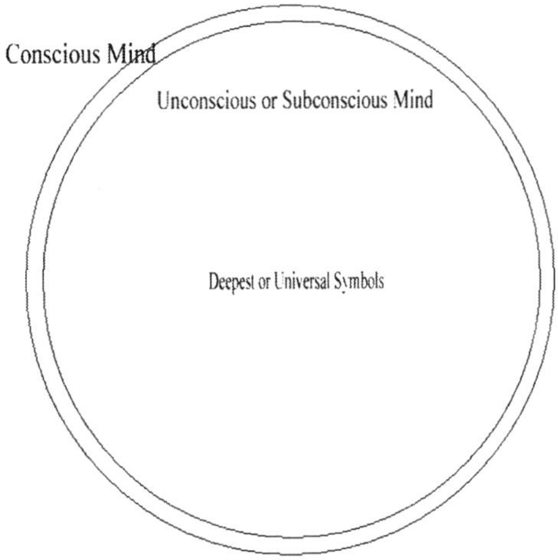

subconscious. Jung likened the two to a sphere with a surface skin. In this case the skin represents the conscious mind whilst the greater mass of the sphere represents the inner mind or unconscious. Jung postulated that the deeper a person looked within the sphere the greater the understanding of the core being of that person became, even to the point where the self became lost within a group consciousness or archetypal sea of Being.

I prefer the use of the word 'subconscious' rather than the word Jung actually used – the 'unconscious' – as the connotations of unconscious today are those of sleep or unawareness, yet that part of the mind is anything but asleep, quiet and unaware. The subconscious describes a state beneath consciousness, but hardly dormant.

Although the diagrams of Assagioli and Jung are inversed to each other, the most significant point of both is the relative importance of the subconscious to the conscious. All rational processes and constructed systems of belief belong to the conscious mind but these pale into insignificance against the awesome power of the subconscious. Asked to walk along a plank placed on the ground and few people will find any difficulty. Place that same plank sixty feet up in the air and very few people will be able to repeat that walk. In any battle between the Will and Imagination, between the conscious and subconscious, Imagination will always win.

Both Assagioli and Jung portray valid descriptions of the

inner person - yet note there is no special spiritual, "in" or religious words. That could be, or even should be, just as true for the diagram of the inner person called the Qabalah, but most works upon the subject are nothing *but* religious in content. Strange isn't it. However, before venturing further let me look at the respective 'languages' of the different parts of the mind.

The language of the conscious mind is that of words. Deliberately not delving into the origin of language at this time, but recognizing that it is an intriguing line of enquiry all the same, to all intents and purposes we can see that words are arbitrary sounds arranged in a specific way to convey specific meaning. For example, that is why in one part of the world, England say, a person says "door" and means an entrance or exit from a room, while in another place, France say, a second person says "port" to convey the same meaning. Yet again, if the first person says "port" it means a place for ships or a drink. Words are a means of communication that takes years to perfect and although making a sound might of itself be instinctive, the system of sounds we call language is something learnt, with all manner of rules that govern subtlety of meaning; rules of syntax, grammar, inflection and modulation.

The language of the subconscious, on the other hand, is that of feeling and concept. Experiences, actual and yet not necessarily consciously remembered, equate with particular feelings of comfort or pain, joy or sorrow with visual counterparts of pictures or symbols. A person does not have to be taught sorrow or joy to experience it. It is just something instinctively felt and known, communicated through tears or smiles, bodily posture or the very eyes themselves.

The moral code, a religious belief, an ethical framework, a political manifesto and all similar constructs, belong to the *conscious* mind. They are all belief systems of one kind or another, built up by conscious thought and rationality. They are communicated through words or expression of the conscious mind in some way or other.

On the other hand, appetites, conscience, sexuality, spirituality and all emotional actions and reactions, belong to the *sub*conscious mind. They are not usually part of a person's conscious thinking, and are mainly communicated in *non*-verbal ways at deeper levels of understanding. They are instinctual and exist just because the person is alive. Essentially they are *not* taught or learnt but passed on down the generations through the genes. They are part of the mental makeup of all human beings within the subconscious – all present, working and correct.

That is why, when the conscious belief system is at odds with the inner workings of the human mind, it can be a time of great inner conflict and anguish - sexuality and religious principles being one obvious example. Morality may war with Sexuality; Belief or Creeds war with Spirituality or sense of 'Rightness'; Political Manifestos war with Conscience or Sense of Righteousness. And so it goes on.

ii. Symbols

So what of symbols, for I left that hanging in the air in previous chapters.

It is said "a picture is worth a thousand words". Indeed, at any one time there is more information being gathered by a person through the eyes than by any of the other senses. Of course we ignore those other senses at our peril, but putting all the data together from ears, skin, tongue and nose, it still does not even begin to approach the volume of data being received from our eyes. Humankind is essentially a visually communicating animal, and the relative sizes of the processing equipment in our brains reflect the significance of images over sounds and feelings.

A picture in itself is nothing more than a collection of lines and colors upon a surface or medium that depicts an experience in life. It can be a real life picture or an abstract one. It can be a photograph or a drawing incorporating 'poetic license' to convey extra meaning. However, it is at that point the picture begins to become a symbol, as well as a replicating photograph, for a symbol is a picture of some kind or other with extra layers of meaning.

It is the extra 'something' that evokes feelings or memory instinctively over and above the obvious visual imagery. For example, a picture of a naked woman may remain just an 'aide memoir' of a particular woman and situation or it may become a means of evoking desire, lust or love. Indeed without such an evocation of a scantily clad woman most advertisements would lack any power of enticement to buy! However, it is not just desire that could be evoked. Anger or feelings of degradation are just as likely to be experienced by some people. It may also be the case on occasions that all 'lower' emotions are transcended by the sight of great beauty which take the preceptor to a height of awareness that can only be talked of in religious terms. That is the power of symbols appreciated over and above the actual image perceived.

Putting this idea to one side for the moment, in order to understand the next idea about symbols let me take the analogy of a description of the physical body of a human being. Such a description should involve the most basic aspects of - barring accidents - one head, two arms, two legs, one torso, hands and feet, liver, lungs, stomach and so on and so on. This is before even the first step of differentiation begins – that of gender. At this level all human beings are identical. Sizes may be different, but that comes later. To describe one human at this most basic level of anatomical detail is to describe all humans. It is a universal concept of humanity.

Differentiation begins a mere step away from this fundamental level as soon as we look at gender. Straight away it appears that there are two kinds of humans, male and female.

Then, when we add size, general shape, skin color, bone structure and facial features, we can add many more categories to our basic model. Ethnic differences emerge that show sub-species within the whole. Yet further refining brings tribal or clan characteristics within the ethnic group, and the final refining gives the description of a single human that makes that person unique. So we can roughly categorize human kind through universal, ethnic, tribal and individual characteristics.

Returning to the Jungian picture of the inner levels of the sphere of the mind, Jung suggested that the surface symbols, those nearest the conscious awareness, relate to the personal experiences of that individual. They hold meaning just for them. The symbols come into being there because of the more unusual, traumatic or repeated experiences that that individual undergoes, and form in the subconscious without plan or will or intent. They arise through life's experiences and cannot be exorcised by force or strength of will – they just are.

At the deepest level of the inner mind, in the group consciousness, are the archetypes. These are the building blocks of consciousness that are common to all human kind. They are there because the person is a human being and alive! The archetypes are the universal mental counterpart to the universal descriptive parts of the physical body, and cannot be thought of not being there as we cannot think of a person without a head, liver or lungs. They are not put into the mind after birth, like the individual symbols, but are there in the womb, in the genes, in the spirit.

The most important part to remember about archetypes is that they are *not* quiet or have no part to play in the person's life. They are working *all the time* and they do not have to be taught to the individual. They just *are,* in exactly the same way as the brain works, the lungs work or the eyes work. A person does not have to be taught how to breathe or to see – they just get on with breathing or seeing, so the universal symbols are there and work automatically all the time, for good or ill.

In between the two extremes are the depths of subconscious that relate to the ethnic or clan psyche. It is at the ethnic level that the archetypes can begin to be appreciated, or their power felt, for at the deepest level of mind the actual description or concept of that archetype slips away between the fingers of understanding to a deeper level yet. You can never actually get hold of an archetype in itself, but need a vehicle to hold it and express it, giving it form and conceptual placement.

For example, the archetype of 'The Hero' is undoubtedly a universal concept translated into many, many stories and sagas throughout the world. The concept can easily be understood - but in its respective settings. So you have the Samurai warrior of the Far East; the Viking Hero earning his place in the halls of Valhalla; William Tell of Central Europe and Arthur or Robin Hood in these lands. However, to try to describe the quality and concept of the 'Hero' without the setting and subtlety of understanding of place and time, and the description is doomed to failure. The setting is absolutely necessary. The setting is the ethnic placing, and consists of ethnic symbols or psyche, and just like the universal or archetypal symbols, these are *not* learnt but have their part within the inner person through the group experiences or group mind, and are born to that person by virtue of that person's genetic history.

Two rather unusual consequences or corollaries are that, as the ethnic symbols grow over the years due to the collective experiences of the tribe or area, then the symbols always tend to be out of date or behind the times, being depicted as historical figures, old fashioned buildings or fairy stories and folk tales. The issues they relate to may be completely up to date, but the imagery used is from the past. It is only the individual symbols that may be contemporary. It is as if the current individual symbols, en masse, become the next generation's ethnic symbols, gradually sinking into the inner sphere as time passes, becoming more clan than individual, then more tribal or ethnic than clan, and so on. Perhaps that is the way the mental building blocks evolve, just as the physical body has its mechanisms in place in order to adapt, change or evolve over the years. I do not know.

The further unusual consequence is that an individual of any ethnic group may have religious symbols within their psyche that they may *consciously* never subscribe to - or even vehemently object to. Remember the religious *belief* system belongs to the conscious mind, but the *symbols* belong to the subconscious. It is the group mind and experience that has given rise to the group or ethnic symbol, for it was the group consensus of belief and expectation that gave rise to experience in the past. Thus it is beyond an individual's strength or ability *ever* to exorcise an ethnic symbol just because they do not believe in it. The belief systems do not control the subconscious.

Remember, also, that the inner sphere of consciousness is not similar to an onion with obvious layers within it. Rather it is a fuzzy merging or blending of concepts, moving from the surface symbols, relating to the individual, through to the universal archetypes at the most central place of Being. It is only because we need useful ways to describe the 'Within' that we devise the categories and demarcations. They do not exist so clearly in real terms, unlike their physical counterparts. It is a false description, but it is a way of understanding the 'beyond understanding', of describing the indescribable, for that end of the symbol spectrum of deepest archetypes probably fits best into religious or spiritual definition, with all corresponding abstraction and obfuscation.

iii. Interpretation of symbol

There is no hard and fast single interpretation of any individual symbol, no matter what others may say! The range of possible interpretations is vast. But the strength of interpretation of the symbol is another matter. It will depend upon how close the symbol sits to the archetype or to the life experiences of the individual. In any case, the range of interpretation commonly used by any one single person may be established fairly simply by making a list of all words that spring to mind by that person, that are associated with the image or symbol under investigation. It is the association that shows how idiosyncratic an interpretation may be. No one else can say an interpretation is valid or invalid for that person. It is what comes to mind by that person, no matter how irrational it seems to any other. If an individual holds an association, then that is what makes a valid possible interpretation.

It is clear that for any given similar group of people there will be similar words of association. Large areas of commonality will exist, particularly for the most common of images such as wind, water, earth etc. The similarity of words across *dis*similar groups of people, show the closeness of the symbol to the archetype, whilst the similar words within a similar group of people show more of the ethnic nature of that symbol.

iv. Correspondences

Seeing how a universal symbol or archetype can be reinterpreted within differing ethnic contexts it is possible to use one version, or one ethnic symbol, in place of another. It might not be so effective or powerful out of its original context, but because there is a common meaning being conveyed, it is still a possible course to take. The closer the ethnic or clan grouping to the substituted group, the more effective the substitution would be. So the substitution of the Samurai could still be used for the Viking Hero, albeit less efficiently, but the substitution of Arthur for Robin Hood would probably be just as effective as the original, for they are of the same ethnic group. One symbol corresponds to another.

One surprising thought is that a correspondence may exist

without any obvious link appearing, for it is not the actual similarity of *image* that links the two symbols but the power to evoke the same emotions within that person. That is the link. A symbol can be interpreted in a variety of ways, all equally valid, but the particular emotions being touched at any one time, however, will vary when using that one same symbol in its different ways. In fact the emotions associated with any particular symbol can be as numerous as there are possible interpretations. It depends upon the context of the symbol as to what particular interpretation or emotion is being evoked. So a correspondence to another symbol occurs *only* when the same emotions are touched no matter if the images are similar or dissimilar. A correspondence occurs when the use of those different symbols overlap or coincide.

One example of this is the basic four elements in western magic of fire, air, water and earth. These correspond respectively to the spirit, rational thought, emotions and the physical body.

Another set of examples are spring, summer, autumn and winter. Correspondences are respectively dawn, midday, dusk and night; or again east, south, west and north.

The great temptation is to equate the two sets together as they would seem to fit so nicely. If we do this then, of course, fire corresponds to summer and earth corresponds to winter, and the associated symbols would also correspond with those pairs. Trouble begins when trying to place spring. Does it correspond with air - or is it water? This would leave autumn to correspond to water - or is it air?

You will find that people do equate the sets together, and will place them differently according to their own inner leanings, for rational argument can give equally valid reasons for the different placing. So one can see that it is *not* really a cut and dried science at all. The use of correspondences is more an artistic or even intuitional understanding based on breadth of experience or wideness of vision. In any kind of investigation of the inner mind this must not be forgotten. You cannot be dogmatic about correspondence or validity of symbol. Of course, there are guidelines to follow and principles to apply, but there is no golden rule or 'marks out of ten' that justifies one being correct over the other. In fact, if a set of rules *is* found promising a firm understanding and interpretation, then my advice is to leave it strictly alone, for in my mind it only shows the writer's limitations.

Occasionally it is possible to find a complete set of symbols that does correspond to a second set. In these rare situations I can only assume that there is a truth being expressed by different peoples at different times in their respective ways. The degree of ease of correspondence may vary considerably, so, for example, the eastern style of astrology, despite having the same number of categories as the western style, relates with considerable difficulty to its western cousin. The cusp times of each category do not relate in any way to the other system and the process is irreconcilable, yet each system may describe any single individual with considerable accuracy in its own inimitable way. On the other hand, one version of the Celtic Tree Calendar relates extremely well with the western zodiac, not only having twelve categories but the cusp of each category coincides with the cusp of the other system. Even each category description, although using a very different language in each system, describes the character type to a remarkably similar degree. That particular version of the Celtic Tree Calendar is a perfect correspondence to the western zodiac, and can safely be interposed if religious scruples are an obstacle to the zodiac's use - and vice versa.

v. Use of Symbols

It is possible to investigate the use of symbols across a tremendous range of situations. We could look into such diverse areas as advertising, propaganda and political indoctrination through to religion, mysticism and magic. However, the point of this writing is to look at the Qabalah as a system for inner investigation, growth and therapy. So our looking at the use of symbols must, in this case, remain within the inner person, the delving into the Jungian inner sphere of the subconscious – a 'getting to know you'.

Probably the most common use of imagery of this kind is that of fantasy. Everyone, I am absolutely sure, uses fantasy at some point of each day. It might be of a sensual or sexual nature; it could be to re-enact an argument putting oneself in the role of the innocent or more powerful person; it could be a wish fulfillment or daydream. In any of these cases, the images brought to mind evoke not only the literal picture held in the imagination but also the very strong feeling or emotions that go with it. That is the whole point of the exercise. Everything is under control. It can be stopped at any point of the fantasy. Nothing is expected to come of it. There is no ulterior motive or deliberate use of fantasy to manifest the hidden situation into real life. It is a harmless preoccupation that gives rise to pleasant feelings. It may even help bring balm to a wounded pride or bruised ego or restore a sense of inner peace and worth. It may seem to have no place in a work on the Qabalah, but that is precisely how those fantasy symbols work – evoking a response at a subconscious level. It is the most mundane example of the use of symbols and certainly does not contain any religious hocus-pocus or 'esoteric name dropping'. However, that is not the kind of visualization course of exercises being written of here!

Another most common use of imagery is within the kind of dreams experienced during sleep. Acknowledging that some dreams may be foretelling or astral projection, the more usual dream is the unfolding story or drama involving the dreamer in a variety of roles and problem situations. In this kind of dream the dreamer is usually not in control. Many are the embarrassing or even fearful dreams that leave the dreamer exhausted upon waking up. There is a kind of free-fall nature to this experience that could tell the dreamer something of what is going on in the subconscious, providing the dreamer has some knowledge of psychology, but no matter how hard an individual tries not to do it, dreaming is essential for health and well being. Everyone does dream - often several times each night. The dreams might not be remembered, but they certainly happen and are affecting the inner person.

Jung saw all dreams of this kind as a form of self-help or therapy. Unlike Freud who was the pessimist, Jung optimistically viewed the inner mind as being in a state of dynamic equilibrium. If the balance became upset then the result could well be a neurosis or even a psychosis. Freud, simplistically speaking, challenged dreams or nightmares. He saw them as a sign that things were not well with the inner person and strove to find ways of bringing peace to the subconscious through analysis or therapy. Jung also saw nightmares as a symptom of a problem, but presumed it was the subconscious endeavoring to right the imbalance itself. Rather than be concerned by nightmares he would be encouraging them, if at all possible.

Just as an aside, and continuing in the simplistic vein, one quick understanding of the two technical terms just used is that if a person has a neurosis, then two and two make five, and the person is upset. If the person has a psychosis then two and two make five, but they cannot see anything wrong with that! As a layman's explanation that may be sufficient, but don't insist on it before a psychologist.

Returning to Jung, Jung postulated that the mind was in a state of homoeostasis. Just as the body has all kinds of balances to maintain, such as body temperature, water retention, hormone balances, hunger and the like, so the mind keeps a balance between the different phobias. Therefore, for example, agoraphobia is balanced with claustrophobia. In fact, his view was that all the neurosis and all the psychosis were present in every one of us. It is only if the balance is lost to some degree that it becomes evident that there is a problem, and depending upon the way the mind exhibits that imbalance, so a particular title might be given to label that condition. In his view, therapy is understood as helping the mind sort itself out, assisting it in some way, rather than bludgeoning it into line or adding constraint and counter potentials.

Going a stage further, rather than undergoing psycho-analysis or counseling or simply relying on just dreams to maintain the inner equilibrium, it is possible to utilize the imagination in constructing visualizations to achieve the same results, but more effectively. It is enlisting the aid of symbols already present within the subconscious, as resources, to deal with a weakness or problem. This kind of therapy is only taking the way that nature provides - and enhancing it.

It is not as if there haven't been several different frameworks of understanding of such symbols over the centuries, yet why is it always that modern man's understanding has to be better than the understanding from the past? Could it be that modern man is just too lazy to look at a past system, because that would also mean work has to be done to place it in context with that past society's mores and religious backdrop and rework it into today's context? Is it just too much effort or too much pride? It is a shameful thing if the framework is already there as a basis to start from but it is not even looked at. The Qabalah is such a framework, worked and reworked but not, perhaps, worked sufficiently for today's needs for instant enlightenment.

Without the commitment to work on any framework, one danger that immediately presents itself is that of empiricism. Just because the imagery is positive and 'should' have a positive effect does not mean to say that it always will with every person. It might even work well with most people but suddenly something might go wrong - and I doubt if the therapist will initially accept the blame. You can almost hear the therapist saying that it must be something wrong with the patient. But within the Jungian view of homoeostasis it is possible that, although a symbol is essentially seen as a positive image when viewed in isolation, it could be too much of a good thing in the context of a person with a particular problem. So an image of positive strength could well be evoking too much of a masculine attribute when what is truly needed, in this particular situation, is a softer feminine touch. It could tip the balance far from true. So there needs to be knowledge of the person participating before any prescription is given.

For one person, due to the strength of emotions when caught up in a very specific and unfortunate episode of life's rich pattern, a particular symbol for that person could well be residing within the *individual* layers of inner mind - as a negative response. Its more usual understanding and interpretation may very well reside at the deeper ethnic or even archetypal level as a positive influence. If unwittingly used, ostensibly for therapeutic reasons, the symbol might just evoke the individual levels of response, bringing more emotional damage by reinforcement to an already damaged soul. As this could take place through correspondence just as easily as direct evocation, so care and knowledge must also be employed.

We need to look at the Qabalah's underlying principles.

3. Understanding the Qabalah - a Methodology

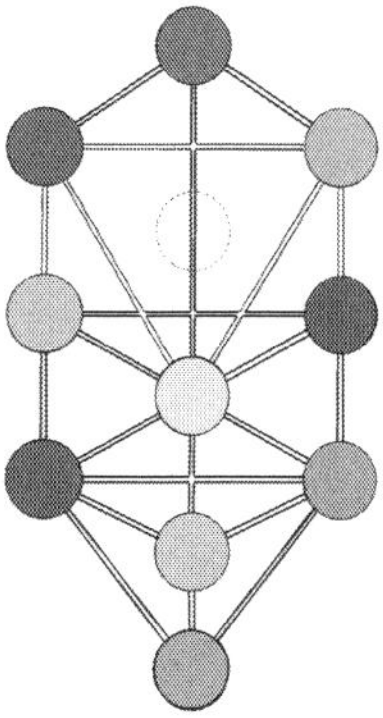

i. Formation

Let me start from a point that seems to have little to do with the Qabalah symbol, with a grid of twelve squares forming a rectangle, found below. This rectangle represents the 'within' of an individual. It encapsulates the whole of the mind ranging from the physical brain to the innermost unknowing of the spirit.

The three vertical columns represent the masculine, the feminine and the neuter or combined aspects of the person. The left [just for convenience] I will dub the masculine whilst the right becomes the feminine. That is your left if you are looking at the paper. In actual fact, if I was being a purist within the correspondences school of thinking as well as the Jewish mystical tradition, the masculine ought to be placed on the right, to follow the convention of masculine - yang - right and the feminine - yin - left. I have deliberately changed this around in an endeavor to break preconceptions and return to basic principles, for it is just as acceptable to stand 'within the paper' and be the Qabalah - *which is the whole point of this exercise* - and then the framework seems reversed to the participant! My thinking becomes more evident when the Jewish traditional placing of positions is compared with the developed understanding worked out in these chapters. Mine is different to the Jewish tradition. It is not *wrong*. It is another way of looking at the 'within'. It really is impossible to be dogmatic with regard to the subconscious. It cannot be held down!

Masculine Spiritual	Neuter Spiritual	Feminine Spiritual
Masculine Rational	Neuter Rational	Feminine Rational
Masculine Emotional	Neuter Emotional	Feminine Emotional
Masculine Physical	Neuter Physical	Feminine Physical

Note also I do not call the columns male and female, for the representation is true of any human being - male, female, gay or straight.

The center column I have called neuter, but it is really more a dynamic equilibrium between the two others, always in tension and containing aspects of both. I prefer to use this latter understanding, even if I have not used another separate or distinctive word.

The four levels represent the very broad grouping of the physical [the lowest], the emotional [the first level], the rational [the penultimate], and the spiritual [the topmost].

The next step is to represent areas of symbols or concepts that can be reasonably and clearly defined. These are represented by circles placed somewhere on the grid. They do not have to reside within a square - they can straddle a line if the placement seems more apt. But remember that although the circles have sharp boundaries, they represent 'fuzzy' groupings of types of symbols. Nothing can be so sharp and dogmatic within the subconscious.

So the most physical parts of the mind – being neither wholly masculine nor feminine, must be placed in the center and lowest square. It is neither male nor female that is being considered, but the *attribute* of masculine or feminine. That is one of the most common mistakes to make. But do take care here, for immediately the strict interpretation of the diagram breaks down. Although this level represents the physical, we are only considering the 'within' – the mind, and not the physical brain itself. So the symbol or circle placed at the lowest part of the grid represents the nearest aspect of the mind to the physical body. It is the most immediately accessible part of the subconscious, the most personal representation of self, the ego, the projected image held in mind of the physical self. Think of it in Jungian terms as the part of the mind that is immediately beneath the 'physical' skin of the conscious mind.

Emotions are usually defined as being within a certain attribute. Hence they are regarded as being masculine or feminine in nature. For example, anger, although being displayed by both men and women, is considered an active, masculine attribute. On the other hand, compassion, again expressed by both men and women, is thought of as a passive, feminine attribute. They are the opposite sides of the same coin. Of course, men can be compassionate and women aggressive, but once again I stress that it is the *attribute* that is being considered - not the *gender*.

Neither is there to be a judgment upon the rightness or wrongness of the emotion experienced. Anger has its place quite rightfully in the wonderfully rich pattern of life. Jealousy and hate can lead to all manner of hurt and injury, but they most certainly exist within the subconscious, and must be 'owned' by all, for if the person never feels anything - good or bad - then nothing would ever change.

Similarly, love can be appropriate or not. A loving relationship is a most wonderful experience for both persons in that situation. The greatest poetry and songs proclaim the truth of that statement. But a misplaced love of a third person coming into such a situation leads to hurt and estrangement. That is hardly desirable - as the divorce courts testify!

So going back to the grid, in this case we need to place two circles representing the two attributes of emotion in the next level and in opposing columns.

It is interesting to realize that there is no clear central emotion, for it seems that mankind likes to place the masculine or feminine attribute on *all* emotions. We might debate as to whether a certain emotion is masculine or feminine, but we still like to place it in one column or the other. Take care, though, not to mix up the degree of emotion with the wanting to place it in the central position. Strength of emotion is not an attribute in itself; it just shows how strongly felt the emotion truly is. So anger - the masculine aggression being displayed - can range from most violent at the point of murder to the least possible challenging glance of disquiet. Love may range from the sacrificial act to the absent minded afterthought. It does not matter if it is murder or censorship; it is still a masculine attribute, whilst the range of caring is all feminine emotion.

Between the clearly defined level of emotions and the mind's projected image of the physical self or ego lies the realm of the psychosomatic. The interface between what belongs to the physical and what cannot be anything else but the emotional, is the strange phenomena of this psychosomatic effect. How much does emotion affect the physical or the physical influence emotion? Released adrenalin, due to low blood sugar levels, may well bring the energy levels back into a normal working range, but through the same process the emotions are likely to take a battering. Similarly, the sudden onset of fear in a life-threatening situation in turn signals the need for adrenalin, in case the emergency demands an explosion of physical energy. It is a mutual reciprocal arrangement.

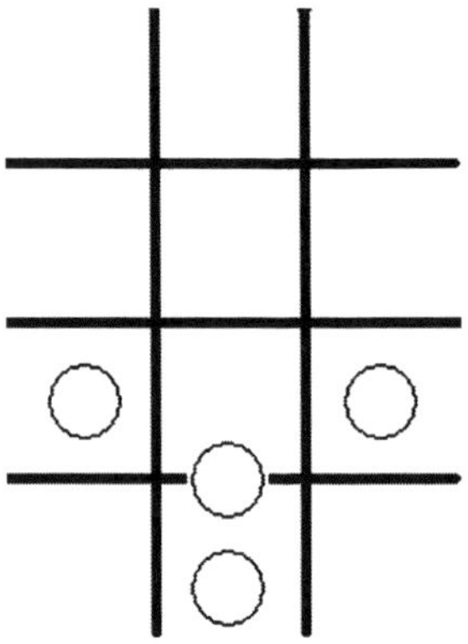

Even more bizarre is the apparent connection between the fears or feelings that we may have for a situation and our state of health. A 'pain in the neck' may be a colorful way of describing a relative whom we do not like, but if we actually begin to experience neck ache when constantly in that relative's company it shows a connection that is both profound and disturbing!

Our grid needs another circle between the two levels to show this working arrangement, but this relationship cannot easily be split into the two differing attributes. Rather it remains a feature of the middle column. So our model begins to take shape.

The next level of circles repeats the pattern. Once again, there are clearly defined areas of the mind's working at the rational level of being that can be placed with either the masculine or feminine attribute. Will power is not the monopoly of any single gender, despite the stereotype joke that a man is never emotional and a woman never rational. However, to be coldly rational or judgmental is considered a masculine attribute and to be deliberately expansive or generous and forgiving is a feminine attribute - both at this mental rational level. I need to say much more than this when I look at these positions within the Qabalah. Let it just rest for the time being.

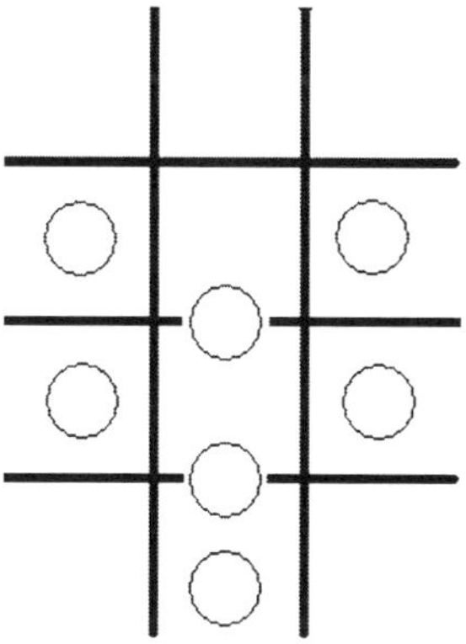

The interface between the emotional level and the rational level is even more difficult to define than the interface between the emotional and the physical. Yet it is still most necessary to include a defined area, just as it was when regarding the lower pattern. A judgment given by our boss or a tribunal, or even ourselves, can have a profound emotional response. Similarly, an emotional outburst can cloud our judgment or move us to pity or tolerance. This middle area must be acknowledged, so we therefore end up with the next level of circles added to the grid.

The top level of 'spirit' is the easiest to show the defined areas in the 'within'. We need both the god and the goddess to be present, so two circles on opposite sides must be a must! Yet again, we know that there is within any person an aspect of divinity that is the most complete reflection of the Divine

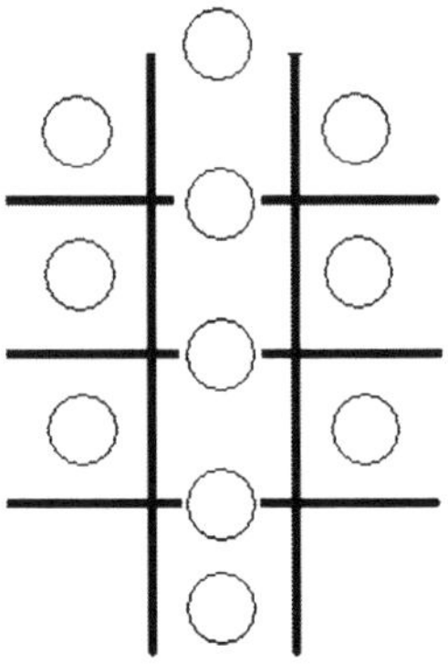

possible. That must mean that it includes *both* the masculine and the feminine, for if it was either but not both, then it would not the most complete reflection – something would be missing. Therefore, by definition, we need an area to represent this highest aspect of spirit that is over and above the separate aspects of the god and the goddess. This is placed over and centrally to the other two circles.

Having placed all three circles there is still the need to show some form of interface between the spiritual and the rational levels of being. However, one of the most difficult concepts to take on board concerns this interface between the two top levels. It is fairly easy to understand the psychosomatic area as it is quite restricted and well defined. It is more difficult to restrict the area between the rational and emotional levels, but it still must lie in the dynamic equilibrium column even if it nearly fills that space. Unfortunately, the interface between the spiritual and rational is so indistinct that one wonders if it can be defined at all. We can see examples of it in practice but the words to describe it are so vague or the situation too complex to unravel that we are more likely to get caught up debating whether something is spiritual, rational or possibly even emotional. The convention for the Qabalah dictates we include it, but call it a 'hidden' circle.

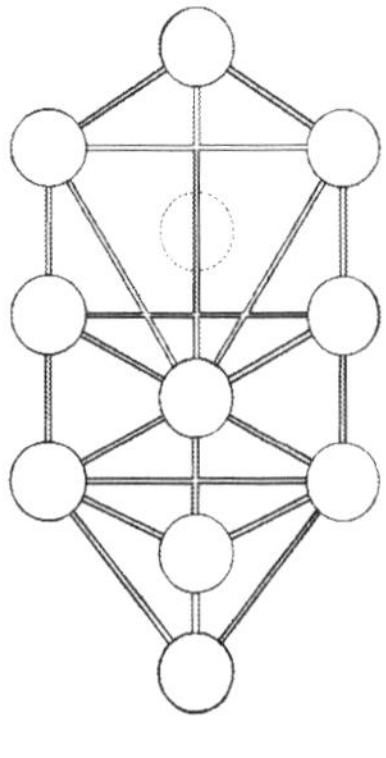

Remove the grid and join the circles to their immediate neighbors, 'pulling' the hidden circle links to the lower more descriptive level to coexist with the centermost circle, and we result with the Qabalah as it has been depicted throughout the centuries.

Adding color to the diagram means a quantum leap of understanding. Later on, when looking at each of the circles in turn as the 'within' is explored, astrological signs can be assigned to each circle that best correspond to the content of that position. The resulting color of any circle is simply the color associated with that particular astrological sign. Be careful though, for in my case the colors are slightly different than the usual colors used, for I have assigned the astrological signs in my idiosyncratic or individualistic way!

ii. Limitations and Dangers

a) False Representation

As a model of the inner person the Qabalah is bound to have its limitations in many ways. It is only a symbol and never an actual picture of the 'within' for the 'within' is non-physical by definition! It is also only one such a representation. Although it might be the most profound we have already introduced two others - Jung and Assagioli, but the very detail that is lacking in Jung and Assagioli can lead us into an erroneous way of thinking.

It is an age old heresy to divorce the spirit from the physical. It is a false representation to intimate that the spiritual is above or more important than the physical, as well as most removed from it, for all aspects of the 'within' are needed and of equal importance. Yet time after time there are ideas of the 'hair shirt' mentality, where the overwhelming need seems to be to subdue the physical to herald the spiritual. As if by punishing the body the spirit might grow or be set free.

Incarnational doctrines point out that without the body the spirit cannot be. The spirit needs to be born into a physical body in order to live. The physical body is just as important as the spiritual body, so a balance should be kept in mind.

How easy it is to fall into the same trap when looking at the

Qabalah. It shows the spiritual being at the top of the diagram and the physical being at the bottom. So the obvious inference to be drawn is that the top is more important than the bottom. We have already said that this is not so. It is also a false representation to limit the joining of recognized areas of the mind in the way the Qabalah does. Who knows how one individual's thinking processes work? There may be any number of links of importance between the Divine and the most mundane. Spirituality does not have to pass through the emotional and rational in order to be appreciated.

b) Archetypes

The same trap can be sprung with regard to archetypes. Jung's archetypes are found in the deepest part of the 'within' whilst Assagioli's at the outermost. With the spiritual at the top of the Qabalah symbol it is an easy mistake to assume that the archetypes or most powerful symbols are also present there. That is not so.

The Qabalah does not show any degree of power of the symbols used but only differentiates the different areas of activity within. Each area has its own depth of being. Each area must include all manner of symbol. Each area must have archetypes, ethnic and individual symbols present. No one area is more powerful than any other. All have the potential for power and use and misuse of the symbols. That is the joy and nature of the mind.

Despite all these limitations it is a most profound and useful model. It is just wise to remember that the model does not explain all and every aspect of the 'within'.

c) The Hidden Circle and Links

The greatest falseness to my mind is the 'hidden' circle. Logic would require a definite allocation. Experience certainly demands recognition of this area. Convention necessitates a 'hidden-ness' or mysterious quality that can only be conveyed by its 'virtual reality' depiction – especially when accepting the Qabalah as derived from the religious and philosophical historical route. The original version did not have such a point!

To try to overcome the limitations, it has been postulated that at each recognized circle there is contained yet another Qabalah, and so on to the nth degree. So there is physical within the spiritual and spiritual within the physical. There are also the entire possible 'hidden' joins running from all the circles to each other. The end result could be such a mass of possibilities that it might as well not have been suggested in its original form at all for it becomes a mass of complications. That is what I have done my very best to avoid! So, I will work with the simple Qabalah, knowing that it is only a first degree approximation and not such a sophisticated model as some of us would like to use [see Introduction!]. That is also why I have only included the exercises of the circles or Sephiroth, including the 'hidden' one. These are the identified areas that can most easily be invoked or explored. The many lines or 'path workings', even only those that convention has adopted, I will leave for another time.

d) Column Attribute

Returning to the ambiguity of the designation given to the outer columns, I stress that this is not the usual approach. I have *not* made a mistake. I have deliberately presented things this way, for I am not a slave to convention if I think the underlying principles can be better explained a different way. Doctrine and belief systems belong to the conscious mind, so to insist that the Qabalah must be presented only one way is a statement of belief and not justifiable within the subconscious setting.

Let me point out that the usual designations along the feminine column – the column of Severity or Form are Binah, Geburah and Hod. These translate loosely as Understanding, Strength/Justice and Glory. The masculine column or Force, the

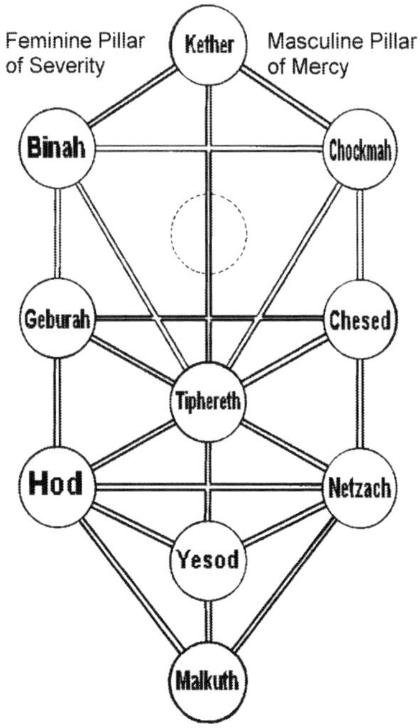

column of Mercy, designations are Chokmah, Chesed and Netzach, which translate loosely as Wisdom, Mercy/Compassion and Victory.

The diagram on the right is the usual depiction. The Pillars, or columns, are on their traditional sides. The historical way of thinking is that the Qabalah is manifested from above, downwards. It begins with a spiritual 'thought' and ends in a physical form.

In this case the energy of the masculine pillar needs to be 'severely' restrained by the feminine constraint as it descends. Force is the unrestrained outpouring and free attribute of Victory or Compassion, while Form gives birth by holding the energy by strict measures of some kind.

As I understand it, in the *present* day in the western world, Strength and Justice are considered more as masculine attributes and Mercy and Compassion are more thought of as being feminine. For that reason my decision is to deliberately 'misplace' the Jewish mystical tradition Sephiroth and align them with similar attribute families; to switch them over at this rational level. For the same reasons I want to switch the Sephiroth on the emotional level also, for Hod is regarded traditionally as 'the sphere of Intellect' and Netzach as 'the sphere of Emotion'.

My whole approach is to follow human experience rather than a religious belief or doctrine. I cannot state this more

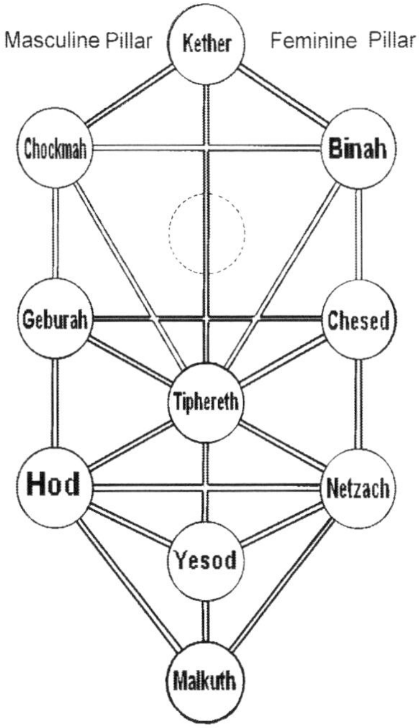

emphatically. It is the crux of my presentation. The exercises are not really for intellectual debate but for experience and personal growth. As the 'within' is discovered or revealed, so the Qabalah builds from the bottom upwards - not the traditional top downwards.

Not only that but, as I stated before, it is a symbol of 'self', so the convention of placing the masculine on the right and feminine on the left *is* adhered to if you stand within the symbol. That means that you have to show the symbol in mirror form on paper, for you would be facing out from the paper if you 'put the symbol on' like a garment.

The end result is the figure on the left. You notice that it is remarkably similar to the traditional Jewish settings, for at first glance the only change is to switch Chockmah and Binah around. It is only when you look closer that you realize the more fundamental differences due to the different approach.

Nothing is set in concrete. There can be no dogmatism in the explanation, for dogma like doctrine is of the conscious mind and all of this is but an attempt to understand and explore the subconscious. My basic principle is to avoid the religious gobbledygook and even the Jewish setting. It is to show a modern, western, possibly Celtic framework of understanding.

e) Different Experiences

Another point that I cannot stress enough is the unexpected

danger of using the exercises for one effect and encountering another! It must be obvious that as the Qabalah has been reinterpreted over the centuries as a framework for understanding and exploring quite different experiences of life, then there can easily be sought a conscious development in one area of understanding, yet an unconscious experience in another. The person who uses the system as a means of self discovery may quite inadvertently find him or herself having a most awesome spiritual experience. Again a therapist may suggest one exercise to help a client over a particular challenge in life and that person may suddenly start to have psychic experiences, which could have a most serious counter productive effect on their well-being!

All of this is simply because the 'truth' of the framework is a means of exploration and understanding the 'within'. The 'within' holds the full range of potential of human experience, right across the spiritual, mental [including psychic or psionic phenomena and abilities], emotional and psychological. What or who is to say that a visualized prayer is a prayer and not a voyage of the imagination, for who is to say that a spoken prayer is a prayer and not just vocalized wishful thinking? The expression of the inexpressible must lie in the domain of symbolism, and, due to correspondences and archetypes, that symbolism cannot possibly do anything other than cross the boundaries of individualism, the cosmic and Jung's Group Consciousness. That is the Qabalah.

If a person has a latent psychic ability or sensitivity then by massaging the subconscious, albeit for self awareness or therapeutic reasons, then it is just as likely for that sensitivity to be developed as for any other ability of the mind - hence the inadvertent psychic phenomena. If the experimenter [for want of a better word] has no understanding of such things or even passionately disbelieves in all of that, then it must be something of a shock to encounter it. For, remember, it is not a conscious decision or a belief structure that determines the experience, but the subconscious and deeper abilities of the mind that are being tapped into. Belief systems belong to the rational conscious mind, and that part of our mental makeup cannot dictate the terms to the subconscious.

Similarly, if someone opens him or herself up to the unknown deep within their subconscious, then they are just as likely to open their being to spiritual influences and encounter the unknowable of the Divine! Spirituality is just as much a subconscious state of being as any other aspect of archetypal experience. It is only the theological interpretation of experience and philosophical construction that lies in the conscious mind. It must be a shattering experience for the confirmed atheist to encounter the 'Damascus Light' of divinity along their road through life!

Let me state it again. The single most important revelation that occurs when comparing different Qabalah frameworks is the realization that a most profound truth is being expressed in these different ways. The acknowledged reason for embarking upon a particular exercise may be to evoke an inner urge to discipline and stretch the self in order to calm the tumult within; however, the consequence for the unwary can be earth shattering. It may, for the unaware and latent psychic, begin a stretching in matters magical and start all manner of inexplicable phenomena, dreams and coincidences. Although the visualization embarked upon may be with the intent of training and self-awareness, the experience may be closer to a religious ecstasy or a sublime understanding beyond words that hints of living beside the Divine! If the belief system and expectation is not in accord with the experience this might well leave the practitioner in a confused or uncomfortable state to state the least! It must be held in mind that, although the intent may be one goal, the experience may be another, so it does well to remember all the historical uses of the system even though the desired use is firmly placed in just one direction. The mind has extraordinary abilities and potentials. The exercising in this manner may have unexpected results.

In summary, the most likely danger is that of complacency. It is one of those clichés to say "expect the unexpected", but what else carries those sentiments? The open mind, with the prepared attitude to evaluate experience as widely as possible is, in my opinion, the best approach to ward off this ever-present danger.

This is a journey of the soul that an individual undertakes at his or her own peril. It is a frightful experience. It is a wonderful experience. I repeat - the exercises cannot possibly be definitive; indeed the principle at heart is that as the journey is for each individual, then each individual must undertake the construction of their own personal and individualistic system. The following is but one such system.

4. Visualisations

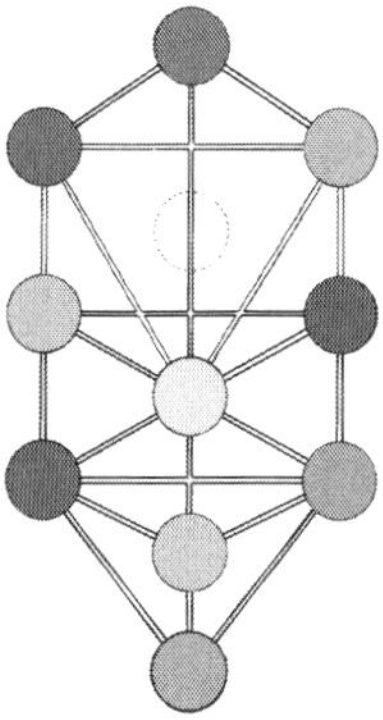

Each of these circles on the Qabalah I will treat in the same way. First I will offer a visualization that I believe can be used to stimulate self-awareness and personal growth, then a therapeutic version or versions follow that develops the main theme. As the traditional way of using the Qabalah during the last few centuries has been the magical use, I will then put forward a magical exercise for that position. Lastly, a comparison with other frameworks, symbol sets or religious understandings completes my offering. I have deliberately reversed the usual direction of exploration and consequent numbering as it seems to me the better approach to personal development this way. So we begin at the bottom of the Qabalah and not at the top, as it is the easiest route for self exploration, gradually going inwards or upwards as experience grows.

Please do remember that these are only my suggestions for a working visualization system. It does not mean it is the only system. It does not mean it is the correct system. It only means this is just *one* system. You will notice that those of the lower places have a greater versatility with regards to magic and therapy, whilst naturally, although there is still such application with the higher places, those of the higher areas have a greater emphasis on spirituality and higher philosophy.

I suggest, contrary to my earlier general suggestion as to how to use the Qabalah, that for the first encounter with the system, each exercise is practiced until the next is attempted. Do not keep doing the first exercise when the second is tried, and so on. That is not to say that the first cannot be practiced again at a later date. You can always return to any exercise to establish where you are or to re-emphasis a special point. It is sometimes humbling or even humiliating to return and see that you haven't progressed anywhere as far as you thought. Yet again the journey is one that you never finally finish. There are always more lessons in life to learn – there are always more onion skins of development to peel away. *Never* become complacent. That is the surest way for a resounding fall to be experienced!!!

I have included some pictures or photographs to help focus the visualizations. These do not have to be followed in a strict fashion. They are only there to help give some ideas to start the ball rolling.

i. The Doorway - The Secret Garden - The Aspiring Soul

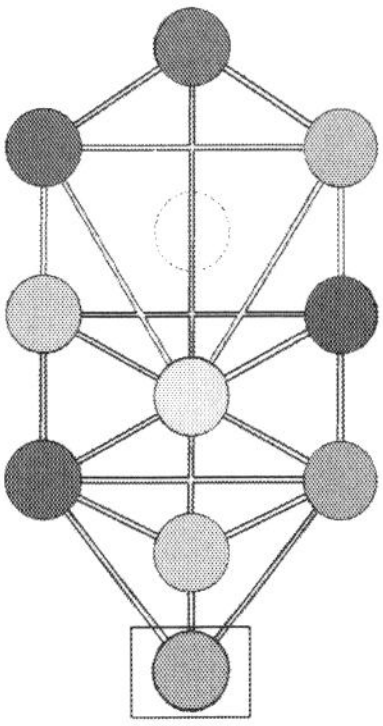

There are various reasons to develop this position of the Qabalah but here I present just two. One is to reveal the near inner self to yourself, and the other to evoke a desire to aspire and grow.

This is the base circle of the Qabalah representing the area of the subconscious that is the near physical level in the column of equilibrium. I guess this relates best to the most immediate or nearly conscious individual concepts or symbols explained in chapter 3, in the section on symbols. Have a care though, for the present day understanding of Ego is more along the lines of a projected 'me', along with connotations of arrogance. That idea is actually erroneous here, being less in the swaggering 'me' and more in the nature of an acknowledged 'I am'. In fact, it is much more likely that this exercise will be a means of discovery - or even humiliation - of whom or what you are, rather than a thought out projection! You must remember that although the conscious mind may want to put its own symbols within the exercise, such a conscious desire cannot be maintained. You cannot fool the subconscious. It will only be comfortable with its own symbols, and these images will automatically be there - if you let them. You do not have to 'think' about them. They just are. Unfortunately you might not like what comes or understand why they are there but that is one of the main reasons for looking within at this level. Have a go, be honest with yourself, accept them and learn.

The primary purpose of this visualization though, is to

evoke an urge to aspire, to grow, face vulnerability and revel in living, yet also be grounded and supported throughout. The more regularly the visualization is carried out, the more the principles of this exercise are instilled and acted on. It is an evoking of these principles that is the "magic" of symbols at work. You will recognize that most of the given symbols are those generally thought of as being strongly ethnic or even universal in concept.

Self-Awareness

This visualization was created from images in my garden at home and from the sight of numerous wall climbing creepers.

"Close the eyes and relax. For a few moments be aware of the surrounding noises and distractions. Perhaps a clock is ticking, a car passing or the chair uncomfortable and the room too cold. Did you take the 'phone off the hook? Whatever the distraction or stray thought, let it come to mind. Do not fight it and block it off. That only gives it power to distract all the more. Acknowledge it and then let it go. From time to time all manner of distractions will intrude. That is the nature of distraction and this work. Each time there are distractions acknowledge them, let them go and return to the visualization. Relax rather than work hard and concentrate. Enjoy the experience.

In the privacy of your inner mind's eye is your private world. It does not have to closely resemble the real world. It is your world, and anything you choose to exist can exist. You make up the rules, you make up your world, the laws of physics no longer apply unless you want them to, and no one may get to know what you think or truly create, for here is total privacy.

See before you a door. It can be any type of door in a high brick or stone wall. It is of your choosing. Your walled garden lies on the other side of the door. Open the door with a key, a twist of the handle, a lifting of the latch or a magic word – whatever you want. Go through the doorway and enter the garden, being careful to close the door after you. That is important.

Although there are many separate flower plots dotted around, most of the ground area is paved by a reddish brown brick. There may be garden ornaments or a sundial strategically placed, but for now your interest is taken by a vine growing against the far brick wall. Approach the vine and inspect it. How old is it? How well cared for is it? Is it baring fruit? What condition is it in? This vine is the reason for your visit to this place on this occasion.

Touch the vine stem and feel the bark. Peer most closely at it, and – because you make up the rules in this place – slide your hands through the bark right into the stem. Push them deep and feel your hands open out to fill the space. Keep pushing until not only your hands but also your arms are inside the vine. Now quite deliberately push your whole being into the vine, expanding all the time to fill the vine's whole structure. Be aware of your legs and feet having entered the roots, your arms and torso filling the main vine stems and your head at the topmost leaves and sprigs. You share the life of the vine. You are the vine. You feel what the vine feels and share its desires to grow and be fruitful.

Be aware of the moisture in the ground and the nutrients that it contains. Draw it up into the plant by an act of will. Be aware of the goodness and its effect - how it brings nourishment and much needed sustenance to the vine. Be aware of the support at your back. The wall is warm brick, giving an infinite number of purchases for you to cling to - tendrils to adhere to. Be aware of the wind rustling through the leaves, helping to draw moisture up and spent gases away, bringing health to the vine. Be aware of the sunshine feeding the leaves directly, the miracle of photosynthesis at work, the miracle of Life.

There is a driving force behind all this. You are aware of the deepest desire to grow. You do not need to know why it is there - it just is. Obey the call within and grow.

As the vine grows higher the view becomes more apparent beyond the walls of the garden. Do not worry too much at this stage as to what the view is; just be aware of the horizons being thrown back. The wind is much fiercer at this level and the wall is not so warm. There is less comfort and a greater vulnerability here, yet it does not stop the inner drive to grow - it just makes things more difficult and slower. Accept it with good grace and let the miracle of Life continue.

Bask in the sunshine; feel the ground's moisture and nutrients; feel the support of the wall; live.

Now let your awareness gradually recede down from the topmost point. Gradually return to the lower stems and gently push your being out of the vine. Step away and turn to face it. Look upwards – look at its expanse and thank it. It has been a privilege to share its existence with you. Respect that sharing and take the experience away with you.

Cross the garden – open the door – go out of the doorway – close the door behind you, making sure that it is secure – let that image gradually shimmer and fade away – and return to the here and now. In your own time open your eyes".

As I have written before, you do not need to know what the symbols mean in order for them to work, for work they will, each time you use the visualization. What the interpretation of the symbols does do is help the conscious mind accept the exercise and the truth of the revealed situation. This will in turn lessen any anxiety about working at the exercise and ease the subconscious' unwillingness to involve itself. It might take a little getting used to but after a time there is almost an air of excitement at wondering what might be revealed. It is amazing how clear and complex the imagery can become. It is truly amazing how the subconscious mind can construct such a awe inspiring world, so full of detail and full of meaning, that hangs together in that instant of time. One would expect the mind to take hours to build up such a picture, but it is presented spontaneously and entire.

The symbols foster the concept of self-awareness together with an inner urge to grow – to aspire and push back horizons – despite the vulnerability that is a consequence to the venture. With a little thought most of the symbolism can readily be understood.

The door and doorway represents not only the way forward into your inner space but also the kind of defense you place there. How easy is it to enter? Or in effect - how willing are you to work? Can you open the door easily and enter or is the door stiff and unyielding?

The garden closely represents your more vulnerable self. When you enter the garden, is it a warm or a forbidding scene that greets you? The type of plants and ornaments, along with their abundance or emptiness, will indicate how colorful, full or interesting your life generally is. Of course it could be too cluttered! The individual symbols may need to be personally interpreted, but the general idea normally gets across. It is not the point of this exercise to do work in the garden, visualizing clearing paths, garden plots or grass. By completing the exercise and returning once again on another occasion you will find the garden has altered anyhow, for it is the symbols working at the subconscious level – on their own – that achieves the desired results. Remember, the more regular the visit the more the principles of this exercise are instilled and acted upon.

The ease of identification with the vine represents the extent of the desire to grow and the degree of aspiration being invoked. Its condition, its height, extent and fruitfulness, all indicate the willingness and fruitfulness of this work. The extent and vibrancy of the roots show how grounded the individual is, the warm wall shows the experienced support, and the strength of sunlight and apparent growth indicates the degree of inspiration and motivation.

What must not be forgotten is that the return and closing down process is just as important as the middle working of the symbols. This base position must be maintained, with both feet firmly on the ground, if the explorer is to be of any earthly use to him or herself, let alone of inspiration to others. The door must be firmly closed as the exercise finishes if the person is to retain their personal conscious awareness and normal defenses in social interaction and relationships.

Therapeutic Involvement

Although the archetypes used are mainly evoking the urge to aspire, this bottom position of the Qabalah is more diagnostic than therapeutic. I do not think that this position really warrants a separate exercise from the preceding one to be used in a therapeutic way. For where does the 'norm' end and a 'therapeutic need' begin? It is a matter of degree and how close to the basic visualization the individual's version is, as to whether it is a diagnosis being shown or a means to 'normalize' a problem. By repeating the visualization on a regular basis the norm is gradually attained, for, as I have already written, each time the visualization is used it will be slightly different – the garden will change. That is because the symbols work at this deeper level without any conscious application or knowledge. In this way it shows that during the interlude between attempts the subconscious has been working within itself anyhow. For this reason I have not included a separate therapeutic exercise.

Unfortunately, there will be situations where a more drastic approach is necessary, with remedial work undertaken before the basic visualization is possible. If this is necessary I suggest the following points:

It may be that the door will not open no matter what you attempt!

Visualize the path before the door. If the path is covered with brambles, mudded or mired to cause a hindrance or a chasm needs to be bridged, then, *in this case,* to visualize the work actually being undertaken to make the passage passable to the door might be the answer. It symbolizes the preparatory nature and sets the precedence for this type of inner work.

An even more fundamental image that might be appropriate might be that of a cliff face being climbed, in order to approach the garden. It may appear rather bizarre or extreme, but as all of this takes place within the privacy of the visualized world, then who is to know - and if it does the trick then the proof of the pudding is in the eating. Who cares what the initial sequence is like!?

Any of the above demonstrates the individual's refusal to work. In this case it may be best for the individual to talk this through with the help of a counselor or therapist, talking about anxieties, inner conflicts and the challenges the individual has to face. It would seem that this must be undertaken before the individual feels safe enough to open up. Upon re-entering the visualization, the door may still initially remain shut, but by suggesting ways of opening it and 'oiling the hinges or lock', hopefully refusal turns into reluctance, which in turn will gradually be overcome. Once begun the way is gradually cleared.

Magical Use

The 'Doorway' is a very apt name for this position concerning magical use. It opens the way to so many aspects of magic that I was tempted even to call it the "magical" point, in both senses of the word. However, I reserved that name for a more fitting position later on, in my opinion. The walled garden imagery is perfectly suited for some types of magic work, especially if a section of the garden is reserved just for this purpose; however, some people might like to differentiate the intent. Rather than keeping the connection with 'personal growth', a corresponding dedicated scene just for magical use can be employed. This is much better practice. The traditional scene is of the black and white temple.

Although differing types of magic are best worked at other specific points of the Qabalah, the work to be visualized at this point relates to the nearness to the physical plane, the gateway to the astral and spiritual realms. Therefore, the associated work is mainly to do with talismans, amulets and the use of subtle energies [geomancy] on the earth plane. Amulets, whilst held physically as the visualization is undertaken mentally, can be charged through visualizing yourself within the temple, holding the amulet within that visualization and power flowing into it. 'Weapons' can be charged in the same way. Ley lines can be laid down by the will in the real outside physical world, created by imagining or 'seeing' their existence whilst in the virtual inner world. *If the ability is real, then the inner mind will create the changes in the outer world.* If there is no natural ability then it remains a fantasy of the inner mind.

Let me offer the following exercise:

"Find yourself standing in the center of a perfect cubed room. There are no doors or windows, just plane surfaces. The walls and ceiling are white, whilst the floor is a patchwork of black and white tiles. Towards one wall is an altar made up of two cubes, one black and the other white. A flame rests within a bowl upon the center of the altar. On either side of the altar stands a column or pillar, representing the feminine and masculine attributes or the Yin and Yang of all creation, the duality always present.

Create a circle around you, and possibly a pentacle or pentagram within it, replacing the black and white tiles within the circle with an overall white background to the design. Stand at the center and look towards the altar.

Draw energy from all around you, drawing it from all directions within the temple, drawing it into the circle and into you. Now there needs be a visualization within a visualization, for as you imagine yourself within the circle, in your mind's eye see a place or object that you wish to charge with light or power, or, in the creation of a ley line, see the beginning point and end of the line. Then, in your mind's eye, send the light, energy or power to the place, object or line.

Take your time.

When you feel you have completed your task, relax your stance. See the temple clearly once more before you let that image shimmer and fade as you return to the here and now. In your own time open your eyes."

Of course, all of this is taking place within your subconscious anyhow, and the best weapon or amulet of all is the magician himself or herself. Such things are only aids in the work, and faith ought to remain more in your own ability rather than devolve into superstition regarding the power of charged objects. They remain, however, very useful tools in the armory of any magician, especially if the magician is stressed or overtired.

Both the Walled Garden and the Temple gives this work the necessary safety, as envisaged by the enclosed brick walls or the religious imagery in an enclosed room. Remember these symbols are working automatically at the subconscious level, giving a sense of privacy and strength, for protection should never be underestimated or neglected.

It may seem that there is a contradiction between the emphasis on protection and the urge to push back the horizons and face vulnerability. In fact, as any counselor knows, the only way to face uncertainty or explore a fraught situation is to feel secure enough in the first place. If a person is feeling unsafe initially and tries to face further unease, then the usual outcome is deeper uncertainty and anxiety, possible displays of aggression, or entrenchment and an unwillingness to face the problem. So fundamental is this phenomena that you can consider it an axiom for all manner of growth, including - or especially - magic and psychic development. Don't try to run before you can walk or you might injure yourself irrevocably.

Legend, Myth and Religious Comparisons

This could well be the point when all those best intentions fly out the window amidst a welter of religious gobbledygook or plethora of icons and imagery. So in order to keep order I intend to restrict the red herring tangents to an absolute minimum. I also invite you to work out your own possible placement of characters and animals etc to form your own set of correspondences in their respective frameworks.

Astrologically, the position is represented by the planet Earth. It is the center upon which the rest of the cosmos spins - from the viewpoint of those upon that planet! If there is no acceptance of the self then there can be no exploration of others. Everyone's life revolves around the self and all exploration of the cosmos starts from here. Visualizations of this system, using the world in its central place, can mean an appreciation of the heavens more directly. It then becomes an intuitive appreciation of the planetary aspects and influence when 'seen' in this way.

Hence also the tarot card of 'The World'. I cannot better the card in this position with that system.

The least dogmatic framework is that of the shaman power animals. It can be whatever animal seems to fit this position best *for you*. I feel comfortable with the horse, but it could just as well be a bear, donkey or any animal that signifies a solidity of form and strength.

The backdrop to this part of the Qabalah system is 'The Gateway' and 'The Aspiring Self', yet reference to other systems or frameworks can bring a wider sense of work through their correspondences. For example, the easiest correspondence to appreciate this is within the Christian tradition. The bottom most area denotes 'The Church'. Here is the earthly representation of the Divinity expressed through mankind – The Body of Christ. An image that is actually used by Jesus in his teachings about the relationship of God's people with the Divine is that of the vine. He is the vine proper, but we are its branches. It is the most physical representation of the Son of God's continuing evangelizing and caring for all people.

A more profound extension of this kind of thinking is shown in the original Qabalistic mystical tradition of Judaism. This 'Sephirah' or position on the Qabalah is called Malkuth. For the Jew the whole Qabalah is a way of knowing or trying to understand and experience something of God – not creation - so in this case, the Qabalah is not so much an explanation of God's creation or the within of an individual, but the aspects of God as God presents them to his people through creation. Hence Malkuth is the most physical aspect of God, but is *not* the physical world. Matter is inanimate unless something of God is present. Malkuth is not the ultimate of un-spirituality, but the holiness in Creation. It is God manifest in creation, and as such cannot be anything else but a mystery.

In the Arthurian legends, this bottom position is sometimes thought of as Camelot. It is the place where the knights and their ladies dwell. It is the place of tournament and training. It is the place of safety and oasis within the greater world where the knights go out to do battle against the wrongs of wickedness. It is the Sherwood Forest of the Robin Hood legends. It compares most easily to the dojo of the Far East. It is the work place in each temple – the Sanctuary – the place of the Presence and prayer. It is the 'circle of stones on the moor', or the 'sacred grove in the forest'. It shows that feet must truly be placed firmly on the ground of common sense. It is 'the place'.

ii. Stability, Responsibility, Faith and Anxiety - The Guide

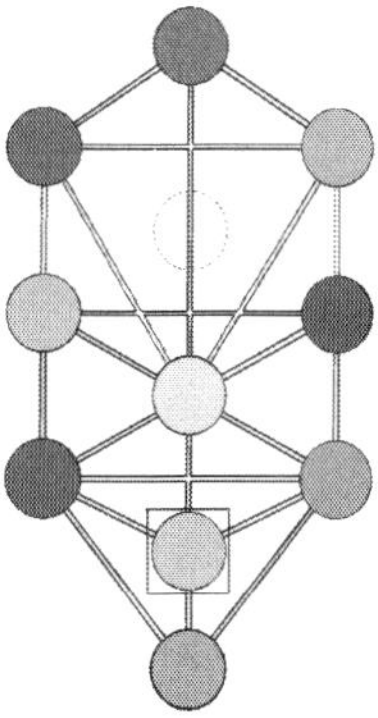

The need for emotional stability is paramount, whether in a spiritual, psychic or self-development context. It is so easy to be blown off course in an investigation or a situation that life throws at us, so in any criteria for growth or training emotional stability must be a number one priority. It is always stressed in the ancient schools of magical learning; it is the backdrop to spirituality; it must be present in one's self in order to help others achieve the same; it is dangerous to work in any of the above categories without it. I present this position as a means to achieve that stability and to develop the balance between responsibility and abrogation of the same. Responsibility, when emphasized, can lead to heightened levels of anxiety, so at the same time as working on stability this position is also an investigation into the degree of comfort or anxiety a person generally experiences, especially in any decision making. Let us see how that person can enlist some help.

This visualization helps us to realize the relationship that each one of us has with 'the Guiding Light' within. Whether we understand this help as the Spirit of God, our own 'Higher Self' or Spirit Guides, that is not the matter for debate here. Those matters rest in religion, philosophy and metaphysics - all belonging to the conscious mind. Although the Journey of the Soul cannot be anything else but a solitary journey, in that it is our life and our responsibility to make something of that life, we are accompanied along the way with many friends and helpers, advising and assisting us from time to time, but surprisingly, we can find them just as easily within ourselves as without!

As said, the main purpose of this exercise is to establish the sense of balance or stability in self development. Emotions are so powerful that they can completely control us. This is an endeavor to balance perceptions with feeling, and to include faith as a factor to life. Anxiety can be a positive thing - but only to the right degree. If there is too much anxiety then it stifles the soul, activity and all that you do. Demons lurk on every corner and responsibility for self becomes a thing of the past! Too little anxiety and decisions are rashly made or even go by default. "Fools rush in where angels fear to tread." In the previous position Aspiration needed the 'feet on the ground', safety and support, and only then was the person able to grow, face vulnerability and push horizons back. Here there needs to be a balance to achieve stability, emotion in tension with a sense of faith - either faith in you or in something other. Such a balance is necessary to understand your limitations of vision and yet be able to continue on the journey.

Self-Awareness

This visualization was created using the experiences of walking such mazes as at Somerleyton, Lowestoft; Wyck Risington and Chartre Cathedral.

"Close the eyes and relax. For a few moments once again be aware of the surrounding noises and points of distraction. They are the usual clutter that surrounds these exercises. Acknowledge them and let them go....

Imagine yourself walking along a gravel path between two grassy areas. The path is slightly inclined uphill, making its way to a wrought iron gate and archway set in a long high yew hedge. As you approach the gate you notice the archway ironwork includes your family name,

framed by a complex design. Before opening the gate look through and beyond to see the path, now defined by high yew hedges that obviously make a maze or labyrinth.

Open the gate, go through and enter the maze. The gate clicks shut behind you barring the way of return. Once embarked on this journey there is no real return.

Make your way into the maze. Take your time and at each intersection or choice of path – stop - 'feel' which way is the most inviting or 'correct' way to take, and walk – not run – along the resulting unfolding pathway.

One moment the path seems to be sloping to the right, the next it is sloping the other way, then again it is climbing, and sometimes it is falling away from you. The sunlight is seemingly shining from all directions. There is no wind. No matter what choice you make all paths seem exactly alike. You begin to quicken your pace and even run for short stretches. A sweat breaks out on your forehead but you are unsure whether that is because of the effort you are making, or perhaps it is the result of a growing anxiety. Your breath is beginning to get labored. You realize that you are now hopelessly lost and there is no alternative but to keep going and perchance stumble upon your way out.

Although you cannot see anyone you think you can hear another set of footsteps on the other side of the hedge. In your mind's eye call out. No response.

Rounding a corner you come to a wooden seat - so take the chance offered and sit down to regain your breath. As you take stock of your condition you feel an animal brush your legs. Startled you jump up, but quickly realize it is only a domesticated animal - a cat or dog or

some other pet animal. Perhaps you recognize it as an animal you had or have as a pet. It seems friendly enough. Whatever animal it is, you get the impression that it not only means you no harm, but perhaps it may help you in some way or comfort you by its presence.

You resume your search for the exit, escorted by the animal.

Together at each junction or choice of path you look at your friend and, as calmly as possible, send out a mental request for help. Although the end is not in sight you get the impression that progress is being made and that the right choices are leading you in the desired direction. It can only be a matter of faith. There is no outward indication that your inner feeling is correct. You must press on.

As you proceed you come upon an open area within the maze or labyrinth. The contrast is quite marked from the high hedges to this open area. Move into the space and look around you, noting what is here and rest for a while, basking in the sunshine and light. After a few moments at the edge of your vision you see, or sense, someone by the path's exit from this open area. They move out of sight, so as quickly as possible, return to the edge of this open area and look back along the maze pathway. No one is now in sight, so resume your search for the way out.

From time to time you encounter more wooden seats. The thought is there that perhaps it is the same one and you keep coming back to the same place! There is no way of knowing unless you mark the seat. Try it if you like.

Feeling most heartily tired, and with the anxiety beginning to return, you notice a much narrower path at right-angles to the main route leading along a much darker way. Your animal friend does not hesitate but immediately bounds along it. More reluctantly you follow. The hedges seem to crowd in on you and the anxiety grows into mild panic. Your friend has disappeared ahead. The hedges almost touch. You squeeze through and suddenly pop out emerging from the maze or labyrinth into a meadow on the other side to the entrance. No gate to bar your exit here! Your animal has been waiting for you with an almost human look of "I told you so".

Your heart settles down, you resume your journey along a gravel path amidst the grass, the scene gently shimmers and fades and you return to the here and now."

Once again the symbols cannot be faked. Although the main idea or picture is painted with given words, the actual images you bring to mind are *your* images. They are those adapted to fit more comfortably within your state of being. They tell you of your inner state and what is 'real' for you. They work within you whether you like it or not, reinforcing the evocation, exercising the trust and faith in the feeling of 'rightness' and practicing the delicate tension of keeping a balance on emotion, faith and perception.

The weather tells you of your general mood and state of health. Is it sunny, foul or fair? The gate and ironwork represents the protection, and yet the one way or only way in to your own special labyrinth or maze. Once on the journey of self development there is no escape or stopping. You cannot stop the 'merry go round' of life's rich pattern. You cannot unlearn the experiences of Aspiration or curiosity. The urge to progress will always be present, or there will be a nagging of guilty conscience until you proceed. The whole process may seem bewildering - a veritable maze - with consequences to your choices that do not bear looking at. More than once you will wish you had never started this self development, or would like that holiday from life. How do you feel as you progress through the visualization?

There are always choices in life and problems to be faced – but how do you make the choices or see your way through the problems? Do you blindly blunder along and let fate dictate? Do you look at all the angles and let your perception and logical mind work out the best course? Do you panic and let others tell you what to do? Notice that this visualization is *not* about making a *particular* choice. You do not enter the visualization in order to return with a specific answer to a specific problem. It is not even just about making choices – that comes later. It is about how you face the world and Life's Rich Pattern. It is about how – in general – you live your life; how you listen to yourself or others; how to make acts of faith within reason!

There are moments when you can take stock of the situation and have a brief respite from life's continuing problems – a kind of Retreat. Although there are friends who may help you in real life, this is about the inner you and the resources you have within you. The animal represents your inner self, your spirit guide, an angelic helper, your power animal or the Spirit of God – whatever. It is a friendly presence, if somewhat strangely portrayed. I am not going to debate the interpretation – that is for your conscious mind! But what kind of animal is it and what attributes does the animal have? No matter what the conscious belief system is, this will tell you of attributes you do have already within you.

The same can be said of the shadowy figure. Is it a friend or foe? Do you really want to meet with him or her? Is this figure a conscience spying on your progress, or is it your guardian angel? Remember that all this is within you. You make up the rules here. Both the animal and figure are part of *you* in this exercise, but the different aspects or 'personas' may be more or less acceptable to you. Whether it is all just you in some form or other, or you believe it is another being [divine or otherwise] does not matter in the end. The experience is what counts, and whether you are helped or not.

The way forward - the way out - can so easily be missed. Sometimes we need someone else to point it out to us. Is this readily accepted or did you fight the animal and go against your 'better' judgment? Even when on the right path, the way may often seem claustrophobic, with no way out, and you become more desperate as time goes on. Did the animal truly leave you? How did that feel? Many times the advising help seems to desert you. The resulting climax and resolving of a situation can be likened to an explosive expulsion from a constricting situation. Sudden freedom or lifting of a burden is a revelation. Normal service has been resumed!

Therapeutic Involvement

Once again where does the 'norm' end and the 'therapeutic need' begin? If the maze appears too tame to represent Life's bizarre twists, turns and awesome enigmas, then an emphasis of this place within the Qabalah can take a far more sinister, dark and contrastingly wonderful result by changing the setting. This area of the subconscious is more to do with the immediate and mysterious, touching on the most common underlying emotions and the way they influence our outer normal waking self. Are the predominant emotions those of anxiety to the point of fear, or just curiosity perhaps?

Anxiety is a natural and understandable emotion if the situation begins to look as if you are lost or trapped. It is an emotion that sharpens the senses. It can be a life-saver. However if anxiety becomes the predominant emotion to the point that it colors the whole of the person's life, then the person most definitely needs help. Agoraphobia and panic attacks are debilitating. Constant anxiety only leads to illness of mind and body.

Funnily enough, if anxiety lessens to the point of 'couldn't care less', then perhaps it is just as essential to look inwards and to obtain a more healthy balance. Only you, or the therapist, can really see if the emotions are controlling you and causing a backdrop problem as you travel through life or the absence of it leading to naivety and danger. It may even be possible to personify trauma or problem memories and influences that are the cause of such distress and deal with them in the following way. I offer the following exercise to heighten the effective imagery and turn the temperature up a notch or two.

"Imagine yourself walking along an unkempt gravel path through a cemetery, at night. The moon is but a sliver in the sky, casting the minimum of light to get by. There are the usual night noises of scurrying in the undergrowth and the occasional hoot of an owl. Brambles catch at your ankles and calves, impeding your progress and causing sharp pain as you push your way through. You have your goal in sight – your family vault, just ahead at a junction of pathways.

Approach the vault railings. They are of wrought iron and depict the family crest and motto above the entrance gate. Notice exactly what name and symbol is there. If you are sure that you want to continue, open the gate and let it lock shut behind you. Gradually descend down the stone steps into the vault.

Stand for a few moments at the threshold and let your eyes gradually get accustomed to the greater gloom. Look around and see the various coffins of

long-dead ancestors, placed on the shelves at all levels. To one side is an open coffin lying upon a more central table. Do not *look in at this time. Perhaps another occasion you can do so if you feel able, but for now walk across the chamber to the continuing passageway on the opposite side of the vault.*

Although you are not sure where the light is coming from, you realize you can see what lies before you. What kind of passageway is it? Are the walls a natural tunnel or are they a manmade construction of block work, tiles or mine workings? Are there any gaps in the floor to jump over? As you follow the tunnel there are various junctions, crossroads and tunnel splits. At each intersection or split you must make a choice as to which way to go, although at all times it seems that the general direction is downwards and each tunnel seems exactly the same. It is obvious that you are completely lost.

Sometimes you can hear noises far along the tunnels, noises of cries, wailing or something being struck. Often water runs down the walls and drains away through smaller holes in the floor. Although you are trying not to panic you realize that you are also near to calling out for help, but you are also afraid that that might bring attention to lurking danger in the darkness. You almost die of fright as an animal makes its presence felt in some way or other. Is it a domesticated animal or is it wild? Either way you eye each other for a time and decide that, with caution, here is a friend and fellow traveler. Together you continue along the maze of tunnels and passageways.

At one point you discover a cavern to one side that is lit by a flame contained within a bowl on an altar. The place is empty at the moment and it feels safe to step inside the cavern and look around. It is a place of prayer or worship, hidden here in the depths. Use it if you care to, in whatever way seems fitting, however, as you cease from your deliberations, you think you glimpse a figure by the entrance, quietly observing your actions. Even as you look up, the figure disappears from view, either pulling back or simply vanishing into thin air. What are your thoughts about that? Are you being spied on? Was it a friend or foe? Once again take to the tunnels, but is it in desperation or with faith that you continue?

At a further point, the tunnel becomes a bridge over a larger cavernous space filled with swirling fog or smoke. Although you are above the fog you can see figures down there, blindly bumping into each other, milling around and getting nowhere. Some you think you recognize, some seem to look like younger versions of yourself, others could be characters more from the pages of a horror story or film.

On the other side of the bridge there is just space enough for someone, with assistance, to climb up from the level of the fog to the path on which you walk, before it leads back into the maze of underground pathways. There is even someone waiting there, looking to you for a hand up and for help to get out and onwards. Decide whether you will help or simply walk on. He or she is not going anywhere, so you can always help them another time if you stumble this way again. Whatever you decide, do it. Now continue on.

The maze of passageways is never ending. Time has gone on. Anxiety levels have been gradually increasing. You wonder how all of this is going to end.

Almost immediately the animal darts down a very narrow constricting tunnel off to one side. Following behind the animal, and with the figure following you [if you had decided to help him or her], you squeeze and squeeze your way forwards, realizing that if you come upon a blank wall then it will be next to impossible to retrace your steps. The ground falls away more and more steeply - the walls constrict even further - there is the sound of a waterfall in front of you - and everything becomes slippery with damp and verdigris.

With spray in your eyes, you give one almighty push and emerge from the tunnel, actually passing through the curtain of the waterfall into brilliant sunshine shining straight ahead of you. The path wends its way just above the water level, in the middle of a watercourse, between two sheer cliffs of rock on either side of you. The noise of the fall recedes as the two or three of you walk along the strange path. Other noises of birdcalls and distant farm machinery take its place. The day has dawned; there is an air of tremendous relief, expectation and, possibly, even joy.

The scene gradually shimmers and fades as you return to the here and now, and in your own time – open your eyes."

The family vault strengthens the sense of personal history, of not being able to avoid the past and its consequences. What is in your past? What has made you? Do you really want to look into your darker aspects? There are always incidents that a person is ashamed of, want to forget or try to forget. The open coffin may well contain yourself and these aspects or memories that you want to put to death. This is one exercise that could very well help do just that.

This maze is obviously not one of a living hedge this time, but tortuous passageways and chambers through a manmade catacomb or winding tunnels in the solid rock. It still clearly depicts life's choices and traps but of a much more sinister nature. The imagery still indicates something of what is happening just under consciousness and again a more detailed interpretation of the symbols can reveal much that is within you. Is the animal truly domesticated or wild? Is the place of power a place to flee from, is it truly safe? Is the person from the fog a person of flesh and blood, your inner injured child or a strange persona or memory from the realms of horror? Whoever it seems to be, you must decide whether to help or not. Remember this figure is of your construction, so represents some aspect of your inner self – a persona - that is calling for aid. It might be the right time to look to it, or perhaps the inner voice advises to leave it for a more apt time. It is not going anywhere else, but why was it presented at this time? If the persona can be recognized, then here is a distinct chance to investigate this aspect of your inner fears, problems or nightmares. Counseling at this point may be required.

The exit can be quite dramatic, and although the imagery is undoubtedly crude, it can be quite effective. The squeeze from

Mother Earth in such a fashion is very much a 'being born' again, or emerging from imagined terrors or entrapment. Even if the experience is not really understood it will still have some degree of effectiveness. It does not have to be placed against any understood or rationalized fear for that fear to be exorcised. The symbols will be working anyhow.

It is a moving from darkness, death and unknown fears into light, freedom and a gradual calming of emotion, as you continue to follow the path.

Magical Use

The Maze is a traditional religious and magical symbol. From the dawn of time it has represented the Journey of Life with all its twists and turns, enigmas and mystery. It appears on stone carvings thousands of years old. It is drawn in mosaic form in the nave of Chartre cathedral and is even found as a modern version of the same in Ely cathedral.

The Maze is also a unique design of sacred geometry. It is not just a psychological symbol, but with circles, hidden stars and ratios contained within it, it focuses the subtle energies and resonates with the cosmos. It is a place of subtle power, stunning in its effects and reach. It is almost a place to be feared, and is left uncontrolled or untamed at one's peril, if you are naturally psychically able. If the potential for magic is present then the place must be used or the energies will rebound upon the unwary. Try the following exercise as an adaptation of the Self-Awareness exercise.

"Close the eyes and relax. For a few moments once again be aware of the surrounding noises and points of distraction. They are the usual clutter that surrounds these exercises. Acknowledge them and let them go....

Imagine yourself standing at the center of a large circular area, completely surrounded by a high yew hedge. There are no exits or entrances. The whole place is safe from interference neither is it overlooked. Here is perfect privacy to do what you want with no thoughts about neighbors that will intrude. Stand in the sunshine and prepare yourself for a magical work. Although you can use this place for many types of magic, today you are here to communicate with your Guide or Helper. Dress - or undress - as you see fit to do this work.

Build up in your mind a mosaic of stone or small box-hedge circles that surround you. You stand at the center with the circles expanding around you, filling the whole area until they touch the high yew hedge. Connect the circles by a meandering pathway until you recognize the shape as similar to the Chartre maze design [logo at top of each chapter], but with a small inner circle pond around an island at its center upon which you stand.

The center is supposed to be a point of power, so collecting your thoughts, send out a mental plea for help and guidance. A shadowy figure appears not far in front of you. Whether human in shape and size may be in question, however open your mind to receive impressions, be they a sense of an answer or actual words heard. This first time is more a matter of making contact rather than detailed communication. Be respectful but careful – and take your time.

When it seems appropriate, send a thank-you to the figure and gradually let it fade from sight. For a few moments rest in the power, bask in the sunlight and appreciate the Life that you have.

The scene gradually shimmers and fades as you return to the here and now, and in your own time – open your eyes."

The Chartre type maze represents a special mystical place or place of prayer that is within you. Recognizing that place gives access to it and prepares you for that special kind of activity.

This exercise especially stimulates the inner ear or listening ability. Work at this position of the Qabalah encourages and flexes the magical muscles in even the most insensitive person. It cannot be anything other than the point of mediumship or channeling – to use the more modern word, and although the shadowy figure at first may contain connotations of dark and hidden malevolence, as the practitioner returns again and again, then familiarity lessens the threat and the indistinct begins to take form. Over time, the imagination, initially running riot, calms down and the subtle can be perceived, and although it must be recognized that first impressions cannot be trusted, connection with the inner or spiritual is being made, and communication becomes a reality. Mediumship is gradually established and clairaudience grows to a useful proportion, no matter what the belief system holds to be the source of that information. The exercise will adapt as appropriate.

The symbol of a place of power draws a sympathetic response from deep within. It is not just to be used for communication. Although the Walled Garden or Masonic Temple of the first position can be used for many types of magical work, here in the maze, work more on the energetic or astral levels will probably be far more efficacious. For example, the calling down of power to heal, especially if the patient is in receipt of some kind of ongoing complementary therapy, can be used in a far more constructive way. This is undoubtedly one form of absent healing, although others will be investigated as we look at other parts of the Qabalah.

In a special place of mystery and power, although it is solely within the practitioner's inner being, the ability to invoke develops. This in turn can affect most of the lower levels of being, external to the practitioner. Invocation is not just to the 'spirit guide' or the calling of power to heal. Invocation can be to divas, angels or the Divine, but here - especially at this level – it is to the elementals.

This symbolism is home for the magician. It strikes a real chord for such a person, and it is recognized that the emotions need to be trained; they need to be accepted and utilized rather than fought. Fighting, in fact, gives them a power to control the practitioner in some way and then the magician can be in serious and very real danger. Emotional stability is a most necessary foundation to serious magical work, for the magician must not be swayed by subtle energies less they rebound upon him or her, exaggerating the weaknesses in the psyche and letting other forces or possible entities gain admission or influence. Even if the belief system does not allow for discarnate entities, the loss of sanity still remains as a very real danger and lunacy takes on a new mantle of meaning.

Legend, Myth and Religious Comparisons

If I follow the same categories as previously then firstly, astrologically, the planet most usually ascribed to this position is no planet at all but the moon. In other words, the correspondence is about the more private person rather than the public portrayal or ego. It is not only private but considered the more sensitive and emotional part of the person. In an astrological chart the moon indicates all of this - intuition, the feminine, the psychic and the hidden or real person not usually viewed by the public. To be constantly aware of the moon's phase or position in the zodiac, with all its aspects to the other planets in the system, would correspond to the exercise of this visualization very well. Although it might be a rational acknowledgement on the surface, it becomes an appreciated inner 'knowing' of influence and effect, raising sensitivity or levels of emotional stability or instability. A connection is known to exist between the moon's phase and behavior anyhow, as police statistics of crimes of passion or psychiatric hospital admissions will indicate, but the visualization of this position or the exercise of following the moon's position in the sky, will heighten awareness and invite a greater openness to its effect - for good or ill!

The animal I have chosen is the cat. It is the traditional 'familiar' of witchery. It is the feminine attribute of the moon in animal form. In my opinion this position could not be better represented or correspond more closely with any other animal than the most private, independent and sensitive cat.

The tarot card I have chosen to represent this part of the Qabalah is the Hanged Man. The look on his face is serene and his attitude is one of complete confidence. He is hanging in a most perilous position over an abyss by one foot, and that seemingly only wrapped round by a cord rather than tied securely. He is either a complete fool or a person of great faith. That makes the connection, for this Qabalah position is the matter of faith or foolishness; to listen to another voice rather than the voice of reason. For, in learning to regard the cosmos by your new values of awakening inner or spiritual principles, the world's view is often turned on its head, and security takes on a whole new understanding and perspective.

An archangel ascribed here is Gabriel - the Messenger, but the Jewish mystical tradition speaks of this aspect of the Divine as 'Yesod' - the Foundation or Basis of God active in the unseen or etheric world, and having a profound effect in the physical. Yesod trains and purifies the children of God. It is the place within God from which all miracles and supernatural happenings are brought about. It is the mysterious forces of God revealing the power and nature of God through events and situations. The images depicted in the scriptures of the Spirit of God as fire, wind, water and earthquake show the elemental closeness to this world. It is the person of God most active in the world that can operate outside of the corporate nature of the Kingdom of God. It is the 'Pneuma' or 'Breath' of the Divine itself.

The Christian tradition interpretation also holds such

concepts as, 'the Spirit of God', the 'Spirit of Jesus' or the 'Holy Spirit and Guide'. These fit this place most aptly. It is the Comforter and Guide that motivates, animates, inspires, teaches and guides the people of God. It is the hidden guarantee of the relationship between God and his people - the Advocate that leads the Church into the Way, the Truth and the Light that is Christ.

The downside of this position is that if emphasized too strongly, or if it is not held in balance with all the other positions, then you see a different kind of derangement. "My guides will tell me this" or "My guides will tell me that" of the New Age spirituality only speak of an abrogation of responsibility. Just as likely "The Lord/Jesus is telling me this" or "The Lord/Jesus is telling me that" can be heard at most evangelical gatherings. How remarkable so often is the case, upon reflection, that God or higher souls can be so lacking in wisdom if the commands are truly to be carried out! Psychiatric hospitals and many a law court will testify to the absurdity or malevolence of the guiding voices that whisper in the ear's of their victims. Of course inspiration can be truly given, but it is also the easiest way to self-delusion!

In the Arthurian framework, symbols that correspond are those akin to the sense of belonging - the Round Table [not the actual table itself!!] or in the Robin Hood framework, the Merry Men of Robin's band. It is the hidden forces at work that bind or motivate the group. It is the sense of purpose and inspiration at work.

Here is Artemis, Diana the Huntress, Selene, the Mother, Luna, the psychic and Reaction. It is a true beginning of inward looking - but can never be considered as being the whole truth.

iii. Drive, Power and Aggression - The Weather Queen

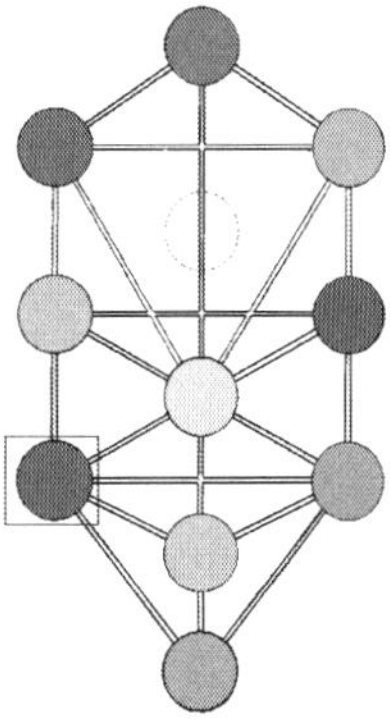

I present this position as a means to achieve a measure of self-respect and to release pent up and damaging emotion, for we are now working at the emotional level and on the masculine attribute side. The universal symbol of a storm is the ideal one to epitomize strong emotions and, as this is on the 'doing' side of the Qabalah, I have placed the person very much in the controlling hot-seat.

Although the thrust of the exercise seems to be that of aggression, remember that emotion can be considered like a sliding scale of degree. At one end of the spectrum of 'aggression' the emotion may be more that of violent hate or extreme anger, while at the other end of the spectrum we might describe the emotion as simply self-confidence or self-assertion. Ambition, goal getting and drive all fit in there somewhere, so do not miss out this exercise because you are put off by the word 'aggression'. Without some degree of self-confidence we would achieve nothing in life!

A secondary purpose of this visualization is to get in touch with the emotions that are usually subdued or restrained due to social expectations or an understanding of anti-social behavior. Unfortunately, just because society at one time or other would prefer them to be repressed does not mean that they no longer exist. In fact such repression often later produces more illness or malaise, both to the individual and to the group that that individual relates to, than any amount of free expression might initially produce. Anger, when justified, has its most positive part to play in any and all relationships. Dislike and abhorrence, if not acknowledged, only lead to a sense of resentment and unease that ultimately causes a cancer of the soul. To deny the negative is to give it power to hurt and maim. To acknowledge it is to find a healthy regard for self-worth, reviewing your own value systems and integrity with the chance to rectify any situation that truly demands it. You may wish to avoid conflict, others might find the challenge embarrassing or even frightening, but the successful outcome that is sought is one of health in all ways of understanding.

Self-Awareness

This visualization is based on the ancient Neolithic construction of Silbury Hill, Avebury.

"Close the eyes and relax. For a few moments, once again be aware of the surrounding noises and points of distraction. They are the usual clutter that surrounds these exercises. Acknowledge them and let them go....

Imagine yourself on the top of a high conical hill. The top is flat, so you stand in the middle of a circle of grass. As you look around you, be aware of a growing sense of power coming up from deep in the ground, spiraling upwards to emerge at your feet. Feel the power travel up through your legs and into your body. Deliberately draw the power in increasing strength, spiraling up from the depths, through your body and out of your hands and head. Direct it with your hands into the air above and around you. Realize the power is affecting your surroundings, changing the weather and raising a wind. Clouds appear from nowhere, swirling around. The wind grows in increasing proportions, until the whole world seems a howling gale. Rain slashes

down and soaks you in a second. A full-blown storm ensues.

The power is yours to command. With a gesture and directed will power you cause the rain or hail to strike or deluge down where you will. With such a feeling of almost bursting with power, detonate lightning from your hands or pull it down from the sky to the surrounding land. Let the lightning strike where you will it. It is totally yours to command, so enjoy the full sensation. Split trees or burst rocks with the power. Feel totally unrestrained to do whatever you want to do. You are the Weather King or Queen.

Begin to lessen the intensity of the storm. Relax the power streaming from the depths, but before it exhausts itself, let it flow from between your outstretched cupped hands to almost caress the clouds apart. Let the sunshine through in beams of yellow golden light and, as they touch the ground, see it begin to warm, steam and begin to dry out. The land is alive with growing things making the best use of the water, warmth and flood of nutrients washed down with the rain.

The flow of power stops. You relax your arms and being. There is a sense of exhaustion or having done a great work. The scene gently shimmers and fades and you return to the here and now."

Once again the symbols work within you whether you like it or not, reinforcing the evocation and working in ways that the conscious mind will never understand.

As you stand on the top of the hill, here is represented your conscious act of visualization, drawing energy from deep within you. It is not a 'head' trip at all, even though it is a conscious visualization. It is from the 'guts', the deep inner you, that the feelings are evoked.

What kind of storm do you raise? Is it mainly wind of argument and thought or rain and hail of emotion? Is the lightening of anger sporadic or continuous; is it 'owned' and thrown from your hands or manipulated from behind the scenes from cloud to ground? Who or what gets in the way - recognizable or abstract and general? How fierce and constant is the energy? All are indicators of your inner passions, pent up and suddenly released.

How easy or difficult is it to let the storm go and part the clouds? Is there any sunshine at all? Perhaps it is easier to locate anger rather than let it exhaust itself and move on. Perhaps it is much more difficult to find a forgiveness or catharsis through the expression of sunshine and growth. Many a person cannot let go of a slight or personal vendetta. It feeds the sense of importance or even the need for existence, especially if such a vendetta is fed through mother's milk. Such examples at this level of hate lie within the ethnic passions of the Northern Ireland or Middle Eastern conflicts, between neighboring counties or even neighboring housing estates or gang turf.

It is out of the expression of the passing storm that the blessing comes. The land needs the nutrients and water just as much as the warmth and sunshine. Rightly expressed, strong emotions are just as necessary as the more socially acceptable gentler ones.

This visualization is not so much a means of healing a particular argument as rather generating the means of expressing safely, even if only in thought, pent up emotions that would otherwise harm and give power to negativity. It is the general overall level of passion that is exorcised or gradually dealt with.

Therapeutic Involvement

Once again where does the norm end and the therapeutic need begin? With this exercise it must be almost impossible to differentiate between the two, for just about everyone I know has issues to some degree or other about anger, forgiveness and self-esteem. The storm could be overwhelming, indicating inner passions being held to the point of self-destruction. Not easily raising the storm would indicate a great reluctance to get in touch with such feelings, rather than a general absence of them. Only a saint has little anger, for even Jesus Christ is reported in the Gospels to have had moments of righteous indignation and upset the tables in the Temple and upset the Pharisees in the bargain! I doubt if man would claim a more saintly mien than him!!

Remember that it is not just aggression that is being released. Although the imagery most aptly fits that part of the aggression spectrum deemed 'anger', even if the person has a most healthy appreciation of anger management and values expressing anger when appropriate, the therapeutic qualities might be working more to evoke self-confidence and self-expression or assertiveness.

To regularly practice this exercise will undoubtedly enable all manner of forgotten incidents to be 'put to bed'. The point is not to remember each and every incident, but allow their power to hurt to be released. The pent up emotions may have safely been stored at the time of each incident, but over the years, the accumulation of psyche debris means a festering of the soul deep within, causing illness and twisted perceptions that otherwise only remedial counseling or therapy can heal. Repentance, confession and absolution, especially if the incidents cannot be consciously remembered [or even owned as memory dims], are not the monopoly of the Church.

When the level or strength of reluctance to even dare look at the possibility of owning anger renders the visualization a waste of time, then a therapeutic correspondence is required. Just as for the Maze visualization, a stepping up or raising the ante can be applied. In this case, rather than a flattened hilltop, a capped or smoldering volcano can be the site that is visited. The exercise needs to be more carefully monitored, but just as regular visits gradually establish an evocation anyhow, by trying to find ways of entering the hill through side tunnels or discovering cracks in the slopes, the process is accelerated. This is not achieved by any visualized digging or working within the exercise at its time of visualization. The motivation to look and try to find such an egress is the desired principle at work. Monitoring must be most carefully maintained if this potency of exercise is engaged, for an explosion of the psyche is always a possibility, and an unsupported outburst may not only be bewildering to all persons caught in the blast, but may cause even more damage to relationships and self esteem as a result. Enough but not too much!!!

Magical Use

The magical use is self explanatory. To bless and to curse is the cornerstone of the work of the traditional magician. It is not for me to pontificate over the moral right or wrong of such a use, but to simply warn of its power. Though not deliberately sought, if a person has latent psychic powers, then the visualization can have consequences that lead to a nightmare of remorse. The deliberate placing of a person or situation on the receiving end of either a blast of lightning or a life-giving shower of rain and sunshine must remain with the magician and his or her own conscience. Spirituality is never far removed from this work, especially at this level of the Qabalah. The Voodoo doll, with its several layers of symbols, ritual and evocation, are replaced by the application of the will against those whom the magician seeks to influence, with a great force of emotion readily available.

To access repressed emotions of a general nature, or especially of forgotten or un-owned situations that are causing a malaise or cancer of the soul, is an excellent therapeutic use of the exercise. To use the exercise as a specific and deliberate magical act of revenge, or gaining an advantage in some way, is another matter entirely. Responsibility, wisdom and consequence are paramount, so any deliberate use of this exercise for this purpose must be most, *most* carefully considered beforehand.

The 'white' use of magic, on the other hand, is equally empowered by this visualization, although it is usually of a more complex design and application. Together with the next Qabalah exercise, the emotional power that is engaged to produce change is explored more fully.

Legend, Myth and Religious Comparisons

Let me follow the same categories as before.

Astrologically, the planet most usually ascribed to this position is, of course, the planet of Drive and Aggression - Mars, the bringer of War. At this emotional level, the masculine attribute cannot be bettered by any other depiction. Any correspondence with any of the images of war or of Mars in place of the Weather King or Queen will undoubtedly work in some way, but not all may be helpful or acceptable in their use. The 'new man' may be most reluctant to use an overt symbol of aggression, as may many a woman. The same may be true of a religious devotee and anyone who espouses non-aggression, but aggression is obviously present and will be working its will upon all, male or female, religious or chauvinist, pacifist or warmonger alike. Correspondence comes into its own in that situation.

The animal I have chosen is the bull. Although it is so obviously a male animal, it comes under the yin category within the zodiac as Taurus, the fixed earth sign. Despite its enormous strength and imminent explosive violence, the bull is such an animal of the earth that it holds a resonance with Mother Earth - the female deity. That is why I prefer to see the visualization of the energy coming from deep within the earth, from the deepness of the person's belly and being. Not every situation is clear cut as to whether it is a male's prerogative or a female's to champion an act of rebellion, aggression or violence. People so often mix up the gender issue with the attribute ascribed to gender, so I have used an animal symbol that has connotations of both.

The tarot card I have chosen to represent this part of the Qabalah is the Magician. Nothing really needs be added as to why. To my mind it is the obvious candidate.

The archangel ascribed to this position is Michael – the Slayer of the Dragon in the book of Revelation. Many Christian churches are dedicated to Michael, especially those built upon ancient worship sites. The propaganda of the Christian church overcoming the pagan dragon was one temptation the old evangelists could never put behind them. Especially ironic is the fact that the aggressive Michael, championing the cause of Christian righteousness, falls just as easily into the symbolic correspondence as his predecessors held. Is there nothing new in this world?

As forewarned at the beginning of chapter 4, I have placed the Jewish Sephirah in my own idiosyncratic fashion. It seems to me a reversal of the basic underlying principles of the Qabalah, and I hold my hand up to such tampering. I have placed the Sephirah 'Hod' at this position rather than Netzach [the other Sephirah on this level], for Hod is the 'sphere of Intellect' whilst Netzach is the 'sphere of Emotion'. The Jewish tradition places them in the reversed positions. At first glance it may seem that I have not switched them around but that is because both the Pillars of Mercy and Severity have also been changed round. Hod should lie at the base of the Pillar of Severity, not the Pillar of Mercy. It just seems to reside in its traditional place.

Jewish mystical tradition speaks of this aspect of the Divine of 'Hod' as the Glory of God. Perhaps it is best understood as the Majesty or Authority of God in our more modern terms, for "Glory" has lost the greatest part of its significance in today's parlance. Even so, in our monarchist country this is lacking weight of understanding and feeling. Yet it is the nearest we will probably ever come to recovering something of the strength of feeling of awe when in the presence of a Being so far above our station, that we cannot lift our eyes towards Him, lest we be struck down and blinded by our audacity.

The Christian symbolism is more open to debate and interpretation. The masculine energy of Peter comes to mind, as does the power of any miracle worker, while the authority of the corporate body of the church must be a candidate for correspondence. Images of any of the Old Testament prophets, especially Elijah and Elisha, as well as Jesus or the apostles, carry the same weight of correspondence, if the practitioner is well versed in their religious observance and understanding. Certainly the masculine authority of the church, despite its Mother Church connotation, holds the same echo of feminine principle, as does the bull of Mother Earth.

In the Arthurian framework, symbols that correspond quite closely are those of Gawaine or the Fisher King. Surprise might arise as to why I have not chosen Merlin, the Magician, but I see him more as a teacher and wise overseer who also just happens to be able to perform magic. I, therefore, have placed him in a position more suited to those qualities and character role, leaving this position to be represented by others within that collection of legend.

In the Robin Hood framework, there must be a far more debatable placing. Friar Tuck could well be a candidate, or possibly Little John, for each has elements of the masculine drive or the hidden forces of prayer or magic that corresponds.

Greek Ares, Norse Thor, Roman Mars, and "All Action Heroes" can deputize here. It is the true energetic principle in undiluted form, however I have not thought of Thoth, the Egyptian god of magic, as being as complete a correspondence as these others. He could be placed here, as some authorities claim, for of course there are many such elements present, however, the Greek equivalent of Thoth is Hermes, and the Roman equivalent is Mercury. To my way of thinking, these two most certainly have a greater affinity to the next level of rationality within the Qabalah than to this emotional level.

iv. Being, Feeling and Accepting – The River of Life

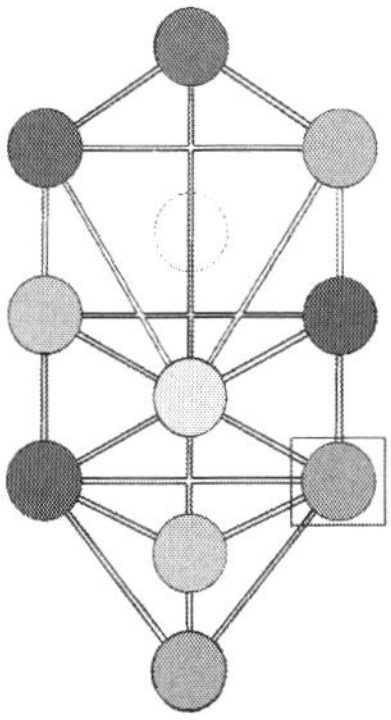

I present this position as a means of understanding limitation, acquiring the grace to accept it – if appropriate, and the strength to endure it - when necessary.

This point of the Qabalah combines the feminine column with the emotional level. In other words it epitomizes 'being' and 'feeling', for the passive emotional state is that of an acceptance of a situation. It goes further and looks at enduring it, coping with it, or even delighting with the constraint as best as possible. It is not a position which, if exercised, enables a greater and wider degree of choice to be possible, bringing in new possibilities that did not previously exist. This is not about choice but about seeing the boundaries of reality as against those of fantasy - and accepting them. Hopefully, it means that situations are seen more clearly, and also see choices that were not previously admitted to. The clarity does not *make* new choices, but leads to a greater exercise of choice already there. It means coping, and hopefully delighting in, the range of agenda that life presents to you.

I know that other positions have components expressing the same, but it is simply that this position emphasizes these qualities above all others. I am not saying that this is a female attribute and not a male one. Don't get me on that one. It is a *feminine* attribute, which can be found or expressed in both male and female. Beware of that old chestnut!

I also find that I understand this position best if I describe it as the position of childlike delight in life all around. Notice I say 'childlike' and not 'childish'! 'Childlike' ennobles the quality of spontaneous delight, giving it a purity of awareness not sullied by cynical experience. It enables a vision of life as seen afresh, not clouded by preconceptions or pre-programmed expectations. The eyes of a child see wonder in everything around, not discriminating between the mundane or exotic. All is wonderful to behold. Any adult that views the world in a childlike fashion has a wondrous gift to hang on to.

I have presented two visualizations for the Self-Awareness use. You might find one more appealing than the other, one more childlike than the other. If so, then use that one as the main tool for development. In the first of the two alternatives, take more notice of the choices that are made, for they will be more indicative of how readily accepting and how clear the perception is of any situation. The second one is designed to accept constraint in a more phlegmatic way or with a philosophical air.

Self-Awareness 1

"Close your eyes and once again let the consciousness first acknowledge the possible points of intrusion - accept them - and then let them slip past consciousness to the common background of subliminal awareness, not easily letting them butt in and spoil the imagery and exercise.

In your mind's eye find yourself in a highland country setting. Upon an open hillside you hear the babbling noises of a brook or spring near by. Find the source of the sound and discover a very small waterfall, releasing the water from a pool that has a spring feeding it in the very center of the crystal clear water. Walk around the pool to the side where the sun does not interfere with the reflections on the surface of the pool. Touch the water and let your hand pass through its surface so the hand is totally immersed. Where do your eyes rest? Is it upon the hand within the water, upon the surface itself or upon the reflections shown somewhere behind or above you? Perhaps you ought to change the viewed aspect and let all three impinge in turn. How easy is that?

Turn your awareness upon the coolness of your hand and notice how delightful the sharp feeling truly is. Push your hand deeper and deeper, but be careful not to fall in. You get to the point of pivotal balance, but before you literally take the plunge, you remember a past accepted instruction that if ever you got to this point, although it would be perfectly possible to enter the water and still live, breathing seemingly unchanged - for you make the rules, but it would take some

time to 'recharge' before you found the strength, energy or ability to re-emerge. You decide to take the risk and fall into the water. For a while explore the sensation and look around you at the pool from the 'inside'. Change your size to suit the conditions. What is it you feel? What can you see? What other inhabitants dwell in the pool, sharing the watery environment with you?

Resist the urge to swim - just float, immersed at that neutral degree of buoyancy and let the current gradually, so slowly, take you towards the exit of the pool and the waterfall. Enjoy the exhilaration of the small fall suddenly swirling you over the edge and along the ensuing stream. Regard the banks and how they seem to rise up on either side, limiting your view, sometimes with vegetation reaching right across the stream.

Sometimes the current is quite swift as the ground falls sharply. Other times the ride slows down and you can hardly detect the progress.

After a time the stream is joined to a larger cousin, yours being but a minor tributary. Now quite the small river, you notice several changes to your environment. Where does your attention fall? Is it the type and number of creatures that swim all around you? Perhaps it is the changing limitation of bank, encompassing your world and enclosing your vision and experience. Does the quality of water grab your attention, or the health and variation of plant and animal life?

As the river flows on you come to a choice of waterway. One is a manmade channel or canal entrance, while the other is the natural river. This time continue along the river – you can always take the other route another time you pass this way and explore its charms and distractions.

The river flows in wide bends, meandering along its course. Other rivers join it in its journey to the sea. Notice the significant changes each time this happens, the combined flow making its own distinctive character. Are there different creatures, vegetation, quality of water and vision? Has your buoyancy been affected?

The journey is nearing its close as you realize that, for some time, you must have been traveling through a delta or estuary. Being in the river you only had the sense of widening banks, not being able to see the lie of the land. Be definitely aware of the changing saltiness, the waves and sense of infinite distance all around you. Rise towards the air and find the strength to emerge and "fly" above the surface. Collect your sense of identity and personal space distinct from the watery world from which you have just left behind. Let that image shimmer and fade, and return to your own world. In your own time open your eyes".

How you view your incarnate world will be reflected in the symbols encountered along that visualization route. If you fought the current or went with it tells of whether you are for ever fighting the trends and influences in life or whether you 'go with the flow'. If you found the creatures alarming and threatening or inquisitive and friendly speaks of how you generally view your neighbors, colleagues and acquaintances. If you are surrounded in pollution or travel in sparkling clarity tells of how aware you truly are. How hemmed in and limited you are or if you are free in twisting gyrations and free fall travel speak of the constraints you believe you have. All will indicate your understanding of life's rich pattern. They will show whether it is a delight or a struggle for you, whether you view the world as a place of hidden danger and threat, or a place of beauty and wonder.

The "River of Life" is there in all its phases. Youth to old age is represented; man-made institutions and constraints or natural growth of circumstances; meetings that change your character; cynicism clouding your view; old age realization of limitless experience still to explore but somehow too late; all release into another dimension at death. By seeing the variations as the exercise is repeated will indicate your general acceptance and growing ability to cope with all life throws at you - or not!

Self-Awareness 2

Some visualizations are designed to inspire, others to hold awe, others challenge, others uncover dark secrets, yet others to heal and so on and so on. This one is designed to help the person to be aware of a truth, and it actually has its roots in Chaos Theory, believe it or not!

Imagine yourself sitting near the top of a rock outcrop or small tor, overlooking an arable landscape. It is late summer or early autumn and the fields are heavy with the corn. It is windy but dry, - very dry. Oft times there are small clouds scudding by that occasionally obscure the sun for a few moments. You are alone, and in a meditative mood.

Sit there and drink in the view for a while.

You can see animals from time to time, hunting prey or sunning themselves. Birds are in the sky. Insects are buzzing by. The world is full of motion and business yet you are still and observant - thinking.

You gaze upon the movement in the fields. The wind is quite strong, gusting around the rocky outcrop and below you the fields weave and dance. Waves of motion flow across them and pass on to the next field and yet further on again. Ripples crisscross the fields of wheat or barley. It is if the surface is more like water than stalks of corn, heavy for harvest.

Swirls of air catch and shape them, reshape and reshape again. Perpetual motion is before you.

Enjoy the sight and drink it in.

Now let your attention be drawn much nearer, to the outcrop of rock that you are sitting upon. Espy a dance of dust and early fallen leaves caught up in a windy vortex held in a corner of the rock. Look down from on high like a god or goddess upon a tiny world of sand grains, dust and leaves and fantasize what a tiny being might be experiencing on any one of those worlds. Here might be chaos or fright; bewilderment or wonder; worlds being caught up and laid down again in constantly renewing arrangements and interplay.

Of course you can see order and patterns to the dance, but each grain must only be wondering what on earth is happening.

For a moment the dust catches in your eyes and momentarily blinds you. Your eyes water and the sight sparkles through tear drops and watery eye lashes. For the briefest of moments it looked as if you were looking at the world from a very great height, with clouds and weather fronts moving before you, rather than leaves and sand grains. It was all a matter of perspective and imagination. The tears are wiped away and reality is seen once more.

Look back at the fields and think for a while.

You wonder what the stalks feel, swaying from side to side. You wonder if they can sense the patterns of movement and the dance that they hold.

Your life is a swirl of business and interactions, seemingly chaotic at times.

Is it all a matter of perspective...... or just imagination...... or chaos?

Let that image and thought gradually die away. Return to the here and now, and in your own time open your eyes.

Any needful interpretation is actually held within the exercise, and begging forgiveness to introduce the Bible, as scripture says, "The wind blows where it wills...." So the Spirit moves where it wants to.

Therapeutic Involvement

This, and the last position of the Qabalah, naturally balances each other. And being on the emotional level they also tend to form the most used exercises within the therapeutic setting. The nature of counseling is to bring to consciousness the emotional tensions, conflicts and denials that need expression for health and well being. These exercises do not need to be interpreted to work, although that is a valid therapeutic use to be used alongside other cognitive therapies, but they work at a subconscious level, bringing a homeostasis of the mind as required.

Just as before, the repeated exercise gently enables the psyche. Choices, as long as they were always there in truth, become real options rather than pretended or justified away. Being able to cope, or even enjoy, the journey of life means that you will have time and insight to make such choices rather than just be taken along as decreed by destiny. However, if past experiences predetermine response, then choice may disappear. In this case, rather than just repeating the above exercise as before, I suggest a virtual overhaul for therapeutic use. Try the following: This visualization is based on the real life physical place of Brentor Church, Devon.

"Before opening your mental eyes, be prepared to encounter a door before you - any type of door – just as before. On the other side is a storm in a country setting. Open the door and step through into the chaos and cacophony of blasts of wind and rain, of mud, cold and wetness, of mind numbing discomfort and disorientation.

The path stretches ahead of you leading upwards. Luckily it is on the sheltered or leeward side of the hill. Even so, the path is slippery and dangerous as it leads to the top where a church has been built. Carefully make your way upwards, the wind gusting around you from time to time, rain soaking you, thunder all around.

Despite the many slips and falls, you finally arrive at the top by the church's porch, but before entering, make your way around the side of the building to stand in the face of the gale. Your breath is snatched away from you. You fight to retain your balance. Your vision is occluded by tears and rain. Quickly return to the comparative shelter of the porch.

Leave your coat there if you have one. Enter the church to find it deserted, warm, quiet and welcoming. Close the door firmly and make your way along the nave to sit in a pew to one side.

There are several things that gradually impinge upon you. The drying warmth and sense of safety; the sense of great age and endurance, not only of the hill that has stood here for millennia, but also of the church itself, built into the living rock. The church is full of symbols, even if you do not subscribe to those beliefs - the empty cross, as Christ, although murdered, rose from the dead; the big bible and pulpit of the authority of the church; the communion table signifying the common bond of all believers; the stained glass windows depicting scriptural stories and characters - all may draw your attention and heart for a while.

As you sit there, be prepared for a younger version of yourself to enter the church in some way and share your vigil. Perhaps you pray together or just hold hands for a while, delighting in shared comfort and support. Now, however, notice a dust mote hanging in the air – suspended and unmoving – weightless and ephemeral. The fact that you notice it means it is caught in a ray of sunlight coming through one of the windows. The storm must have passed on as you sat here.

Quietly, so as not to disturb the peace, get up, say your goodbyes [if necessary] for now, and leave the building, gently closing the door of the church behind you. Indeed the last clouds are scudding by, pursued by invisible gusts of wind. Return to the windward side of the church, yet this time bask in the sunshine and vastness of vision that opens before you. As the warmth penetrates, let your consciousness leave that place, return to the here and now, and in your own time open your eyes."

Should the above be too much at odds with the individual's religious scruples, then obviously the image of the church could be counter-productive. In that instance, I suggest the correspondence of a grotto towards the top of the hill. Here, the entrance is attained by ducking through a curtain of water streaming from above, whilst inside, the grotto is filled with a still and very deep pool, and the walls contain sparkling clusters of crystals. The magical or fairy grotto aspect is highlighted that may substitute for the church, yet retaining a sense of other-worldly 'special-ness' – that most necessary extra ingredient.

The exercise not only allows the pain of past events to be relived [even though not really remembered], but also links it to a healing place of the subconscious. The acceptance and dealing with it eventually frees the person of its constricting or imprisoning power. Events are not exorcised but put to rest, as resources within are brought into play.

In particular, the younger version of you represents the injured persona that is still in pain. This is especially so if that persona is a child or teenager, for the ability of such a person at a tender age to defend itself and cope with life's brickbats is quite limited. A child may well forget a painful experience as part of a learnt defense mechanism, but that is no guarantee that that pain is not still hurting somewhere deep within. Often counseling is an attempt to heal the past pain, bringing an adult's ability and understanding to the situation. In this exercise, even though only the subconscious holds the memory of the event and brings the hurt child to the visualization, the adult can bring a comfort to the child, easing its anguish in this symbolic but direct way.

The dust mote represents your self, held for the moment in life giving light. The peace is a place or resource within you, giving you the chance to review the pain of the past. The high viewpoint revisited shows that you have a renewed vision of life and choices that can be made. All these are evoked and strengthened as the exercise is repeated.

Magical Use

One formal description of Magic is "Be, in order to Become". Not only is understanding of a dynamic situation, person or place sought by identification with it [whatever "it" is], but it is also a remedy or way of manipulating or influencing that situation, person or place. That is magic. This position of the Qabalah balances the previous one as "Form" to its "Force".

Practicing the self-awareness exercise strengthens the ability to identify with life and to appreciate its subtle forces that shape our lives. However, just as the previous exercise can be adapted to magical use, by changing the 'outward' or corresponding symbols to blast or bless specific people or situations, then most certainly this one can be adapted as well. Courage or faith in one's use of correspondences gradually grows, as will the ability to make significant change at Will.

I suggest that the setting be kept of the initial use of the bubbling stream and spring. However, instead of entering the pool and letting yourself be swept away by the current, look into the crystal clarity of the pool and see not only your hand, the pools inhabitants and the surface reflection, but also a picture or reflection of the situation that you seek knowledge about. It is a form of divination, but not about the future or foretelling, but rather a forth-telling or understanding of a *present* situation. It is an exercise of clairvoyance using the inner mind rather than external paraphernalia. If desired, the imagery seen can even be entered into exactly as for the pool and stream, but this time the situation can be explored as in an unfolding real life drama or as a 'photographic still'.

The magical object of the exercise is to understand all the implications, ins and outs of the situation before applying the power to change things. You can see what needs to be done to alter it to suit your purposes. Once sure of what you want, you then hold that image as constantly as possible and 'pour' energy into it to 'set it' or make it into real life. "Be - in order to Become". Once the picture is established it is empowered into existence or manifested.

Note that there is no real need to bring the two together in a single visualization. The working of magic is achieved because you are a whole person with the power or 'force' from the masculine attribute exercise combining with the 'form' of the feminine exercise. However, for some people the combining is a natural progression and necessary step to Change. In this case, the combination can be achieved if you create a vision within a vision. Use a miniature encapsulated world of the deliberately changed situation held within a sphere or ball [Form], then see it released it into the air by the magician standing upon the flattened hilltop of the previous exercise [Force], pouring energy into it as it floats before you.

As stated, these two positions of the Qabalah balance each other in many ways, magic being no exception. Providing the ability is potential, and not just fantasized, its gradual growth is enabled through the use of *both* exercises. Form without Force is of no real use, and Force without Form is a danger to everyone. The regular use of both exercises will develop the Form and Force.

Be careful! Once again I caution concerning the use of this exercise in magic. The consequences of interference may be underestimated. The debt of involvement may be beyond your ability to bear. Take *great* care before use!!!

Legend, Myth and Religious Comparisons

Astrologically, the planet that must be the correspondence here is the planet of 'Love of Life' – Venus. Not all women are beings of love, yet womankind best describes this attribute like no other. The tarot card I have chosen must surely be the Priestess. She represents the feminine divinity upon earth within the Mother Earth understanding or religious framework, to represent her voice to her children, caring for them, healing them and making them fecund.

The animal I have chosen is the Swan or Deer, epitomizing the grace and delicacy of the feminine.

All heroines fit the correspondence just as all heroes fit the next position. But note it is the stylized heroine - the one needing protection, rather than a female hero who is being spoken of here. Hence, some characters fit the bill better than others, but still, Mary from the Gospels, Maid Marion from the Robin Hood stories, Nimue or the Lady of the Lake from the Arthurian legends, Trinity from the Matrix films [although she borders upon the female hero], Venus the Goddess of Love and Aphrodite, can all be used.

The Christian correspondences not only include Mary but also the healing stories, as they present the nurturing pastoral care of Mother Church, possibly manipulating or 'caring' for the flock as Mother Church know best!

Noting that I switched the places of the Sephirah at this level even though it seems to reside in its traditional place, the Jewish mystical tradition calls this position Netzach or the "Victory of God" - the Beauty Triumphant. I do not think that the tradition is seeing God as some kind of substitute female persona, but rather this might best be understood as the aspect of God that knows no limit to his care for his people. Such Old Testament books as Hosea predate and prepare the way for the parables of Christ's teaching of the unconditional love of God, and the ultimate sacrifice that was to be paid for all people. Just as the Glory of God cannot really be appreciated by human kind today, neither can the Victory or Beauty of God be appreciated fully either. Revelation has its day and new understandings take their place.

v. The Perfect Balance Point - At One'ment

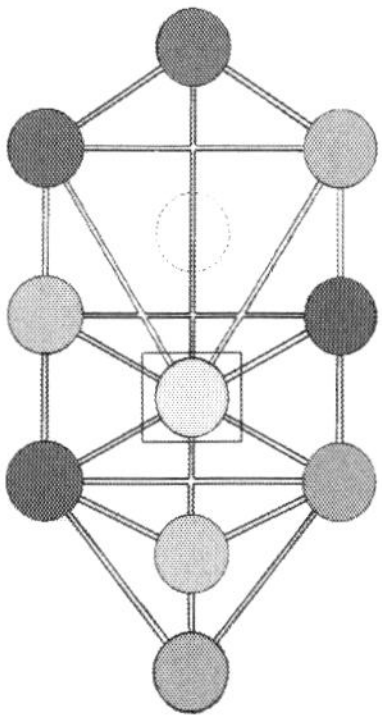

Returning to the past section regarding the limitations of the Qabalah framework, remember I wrote that it is a fallacy to think of 'spiritual' as being more important than 'physical'. Unfortunately, the Qabalah symbol must be presented in a two dimensional diagram on a surface. That means that the 'spiritual' positions are usually drawn higher up on that surface than the 'physical' ones, and the resulting connotation leaves you with a hierarchical understanding between the two. As stated that is not the actual case. All aspects of a person are essential in order for that person to be alive and so one cannot be more important than another. Sometimes it is impossible to differentiate where one aspect devolves into another anyhow.

The development of this fifth focus of the 'within' holds the key to the tension between all aspects of the person, such as being 'grounded' and 'spiritually aware', or, in other words, not 'too heavenly minded to be of any earthly use'! It also balances the emotional and the rational and combines both the feminine and the masculine. So if there is one position that incorporates something of all the others, and can thus lay claim to be the most significant [rather than the most important] point of the system, then it is this point of equilibrium - the Perfect Balance Point - Atonement.

An extremely important part of a person's make-up is their sexuality. It is such a fundamental part of the inner person that it cannot be neglected in a work of this kind. No matter what the conscious stance may be to sexuality and sexual orientation the inner person's feelings and appetites cannot be quashed, even if that person holds to a very strict outer religious, ethic or moral code of behavior. The subconscious demands to be heard and can cause extreme discomfort if the inner and outer person is not in harmony. Moreover, spirituality is so closely allied to sexuality that the more common expression of that alliance is one of overlapping experience and anticipation. The denial of sexual expression can just as easily lead to a twisted spirituality as can an over indulgence or misuse of the same.

Despite living in a relatively liberated society and time, sexual mores still tend to be a private matter. It is an amusing idea to some people yet a most uncomfortable idea to others, but the much more common experience is the anxiety in contemplating the possibility that God is 'looking on' as some kind of voyeur! That will bring a flush of shame to most people's faces! And yet, if we have a living faith, absolutely nothing is hidden from the Divine and everything we do affects our relationship with God. So for such a fundamental drive and activity not to be taken into account in any exposition on the 'spiritual way' is a gross oversight. Yet such an oversight is more likely to be the norm rather than the exception within the main religions of today. I wonder why.

Religiously speaking, and not just within the Christian religion, the comparison of the earthly relationship between a man and a woman is often the teaching point of the potential depth of feeling and intimacy that can exist between human kind and the Divine. However, this is not a treatise on such a doctrine. I just wish to leave it as a possible insight into the sacredness of sex and sexual behavior within the celestial marriage of heaven and earth, and focus on the human experience of the marriage of the many parts of each individual, with the need to constantly review and hold the dynamic tension of the whole. You may think I am cheating but that is a kind of marriage that affects everyone on this path, and not just the 'religious' few.

Once again I try to use only the most ethnic and universal symbols possible, and what can be more universal than a man and woman making love. The starting point of this exercise may vary as to gender or mood but I suggest you begin by using the one that is ascribed to your own gender. On another occasion try the other beginning point. Ring the changes until you are comfortable with either. In fact, ideally use both within the same exercise, for, although you make up the rules in this inner world and have the right to follow your inclination, the aim of this exercise is to balance the masculine and feminine attributes. To exercise both gender starting points may seem like stretching fantasy unnecessarily too far, but it cannot help but assist any individual to accommodate both attributes in a way that preserves privacy and confidentiality, yet stretches the transsexual awareness.

Self-Awareness

This exercise was created by combining the experiences of exploring Dartmoor and the New Forest areas.

"Close your eyes and once again let the consciousness move from the possible points of intrusion to the picture gradually developing in the inner world of the subconscious.

In your mind's eye imagine yourself as a woman, and find yourself in a cave or grotto, quite nude. The cave is far from dark for, everywhere you look, candles fill the place with warmth and light showing you to be in a womb shaped cave. The whole place sparkles with tiny scintillating stars of crystal origin or prismatic color in water droplets hanging from stalactites that cover the ceiling or that drop upon stalagmites that cover the floor - color that almost defeats the eye's perception and awareness. It is safe; it is warm; it is so still and magical. Your whole body is alert to the slightest sense and signal. It is a most sensual experience held in that moment. It is also quite sexual. Be very aware of your body. Because you create your inner world as you like it to be, change your body if you like to – your height, weight, hair or shape. This is one make-over that does not require the surgeon's knife, is instantaneous and meets your full approval! Delight in being a woman, aware of your body and its seductive beauty and form.

To some degree you must break the spell for more light filters down from the tunnel that stretches ahead of you, beckoning you forwards and upwards. Move up and along the tunnel until you can see the outside world opening out above you. Emerge from the ground and discover a wood that extends in all directions from the cave mouth. A golden afternoon of dappled sunshine greets you, green leaf, lazy insects flying around you and a grassy path to follow.

Quite, unconcerned about your nakedness, walk along the unfolding pathway, all the while listening to the activity of the animals, birds and insects around you. Nature is abundant and very busy. Mother Earth is prolific and fecund.

Take special notice of the silky touch of the grass beneath your feet. Let the warm air caress your skin. Dance along if you want, for there is no one else to worry about. Privacy is complete.

The path opens out to a sward of green before a delightful pool of water. The land rises in a cliff the other side, and water falls from quite a height into the pool from a very small stream cascading down the cliff face, ruffling the surface and destroying reflections. The temptation is too great, so step into the water, catching your breath at its sharp coolness, swim to the shower and play in its fall. The pressure is enough to lightly sting but not enough to hurt and spoil your fun. Hide behind the curtain of water and watch the world from your rainbow'ed aspect. Wait in anticipation.

It is no surprise when you espy a naked man slowly approaching the pool from further down the pathway, so spy on him for a while from your hidden vantage point. Take note of his body, his muscles and stance. He unknowingly shows his power and confidence in every gesture and step. You realize you know him, although the actual recognition rests deep in your memory or subconscious. There is no embarrassment – just a sense of fun and privilege to look upon him, undiscovered as yet.

He looks towards the fall, sees you, laughs, enters the pool and joins you in your swim. Hold hands and float there together for a while.

....

Leave that image and gradually build up another picture.

....

In your mind's eye imagine yourself as a man, and find yourself standing upon a rock ledge high on a moor somewhere. You are nude. There is absolutely no one – not a soul to be seen in any direction.

As you face the sunshine be aware of how warming it is on your skin, particularly your face and chest. It seems to enter deeper than just the surface skin, reaching right down into your sinews. Feel the air passing as a warm wind across your body, caressing and stimulating at the same time, moving the hairs of your body so it feels so sensual and intimate. Be very aware of

your body, and as you create this inner world that you find yourself in, change your body to suit your desires. Perhaps be taller, broader, more muscular, or have even more hair. You cannot help but be aware of your sexual nature. If it is right then let there be a response to the sensual and sexual experience. Stand there and delight in being who you now are and feel something of your power and strength.

Look around you and know that although the land seems empty, it is in fact teeming with life of all kinds, of animal, bird and insect. Listen to the wind, the call of a bird, the buzz of insects' wings. Catch the glint of reflected sunlight off a crystalline fracture in the granite. See the light dancing off surface water in the distance. Although Life is abundant in this seeming emptiness, your attention is caught by the clouds, the blueness of the sky and the unending sense of distance opening up above you. Hold that moment for a while – even holding your breath in case you break the spell.

Relax and look at the land near by. There is a spring and small issuing stream near at hand. Follow the stream through the heather, brushing aside the plant stems scratching your legs as you push through. Catch sight of an adder sunning itself on a large boulder and walk on by before you disturb its slumber. A buzzard flies overhead, screeching a welcome or complaint!

In short order the land drops away, the stream gathering speed as it tumbles down its bed. The heather and moor give ground to larger and larger rocks, bracken, gorse and grasses. All at once the stream takes great leaps down precipitous drops, following its own rocky path to follow its destiny to the far, far sea. A path is discernable to one side so change direction and follow the path as it descends into a leafy valley and wood.

The air is heavier here, warmer and moist. You slow your progress and admire the trees, feeling the silkiness or almost satin texture of the grass beneath your feet.

All at once you emerge into a clearing in which a large pool spreads itself in leafy shade. Your stream descends as a high waterfall into the pool at its farthest side. Then it gradually dawns upon you that a beautiful woman is hiding behind the fall, looking at you in brazen fashion. You realize you recognize the woman, although the actual recognition rests deep in your memory or subconscious. You laugh and enter the pool, gasping as its coldness grips your body. Swim to the woman, hold hands and float there together for a while.

....

Now as either the man or woman or as both, together swim to the shore and wade out onto the grass. Once again be aware of the texture and softness of the grass, the animals that look upon you, the buzz of Life all around. Hand in hand leave the path and walk amongst the trees, finding a moss covered bower beneath towering beeches.

Gently, oh so gently, begin to make love in that secret place, coming together in shared delight and gradually letting go of conscious control. In the merging of your bodies it seems as if there is a merging with the land. The moss and ground enfolds you; the trees shield and cover you; you no longer know where the ground, trees, moss or your bodies stop. You become one with it all and climax in such profound harmony, that male and female combine; Earth unites with the Sky; all Nature is One.

Hold that moment for as long as you can then - extremely slowly - let your consciousness slip away from the bower. Return to your physical body, and in your own time open your eyes".

The evocation is that of harmony, intimacy, communion and awareness of all parts of your being and consciousness. Human beings are a mixture of spiritual, physical, rational and emotional. There is male and female in all of us as masculine and feminine attribute. All of this needs to be held in balance, not denying any part of it nor emphasizing one part at the expense of another. Perhaps an impossible ideal, but this is one to strive for nevertheless. That is Jung's 'Individuation' or emotional maturity, spiritual depth and attainment.

The symbols encountered along the route of this exercise tell you of issues or points to ponder upon. Was it easier to visualize yourself as the man or the woman? Does this mean that you are more at home with the masculine or the feminine aspect? Do you need to seek a closer balance? Did you find the whole too embarrassing or even impossible to sustain? Think well upon your answers.

As far as I am aware there is nothing in the exercise that can dictate as to gender orientation or appropriate or inappropriate symbolism to incline to lesbian, gay or straight involvement. The *attribute* is being explored rather than sexual orientation. Sexuality is part of our experience, and due to its profundity, is a natural expression of spiritual atonement. That is why some religions have so casually taken it up! I truly believe it is the puritan streak or the idea that sex is somehow dirty or shameful, that is the unhealthy aberration.

Therapeutic Involvement

Because the Self Awareness exercise endeavors to attain the perfect balance, I was tempted not to include a separate exercise under this heading. However, I am aware that mainly due to society's prejudices or people's upbringing in general, images of naked people making love, even in the utter privacy of the inner mind, may cause embarrassment or stumbling blocks that are counter productive to the evocation. I offer the following as a less provocative alternative. It is also easily adapted to include specific features of therapy, bringing adult resources to memories and pain incurred at an earlier younger time. That part of the exercise can always be omitted, if felt unnecessary. The exercise is still one to unite and balance the various aspects of the whole.

"Open your mental eyes and find yourself on a country walk. It can be from a real time and physical place or one contrived totally within your imagination. Walk along the path enjoying the sunshine, views and images of Life all around you. No one else is present. You are totally alone.

Somewhere ahead of you is a special place that you visit from time to time, for it holds a magic of rest, power and 'something extra' that is difficult to describe, but is an essential part of the experience. Also you know you will be safe there, for there is always a very dear friend protecting the way from unwanted intrusion or observation.

Slowing down you see your friend, a large feline animal, guarding the way and eyeing you expectantly. Approach the animal, acknowledge the friendship and privilege you have with the animal, and gradually pass on by.

Immediately to one side you see the entrance to your special meadow and special place, for in the center of the meadow is a very special tree. It can be any type of tree – but it is <u>your</u> special tree. There can be a stream near by, or a pool or lake. There can even be a cliff or escarpment falling away further on, for although that mix of features may be a nigh impossibility in real physical life, remember you make up the rules in this inner world.

Approach the tree and lay your hands upon its bark. You know from past experience how easy the next part is, so gently, gently push your hands into the trunk – then your arms – and finally step completely into the trunk.

Expand your consciousness so your feet and legs move down deep into the roots to hold fast in the rock, soil, moisture and earth. Expand your arms and head to fill the branches and topmost twigs and leaves, until you fill the whole tree. Indeed you share the life of the tree – you become the tree.

Draw up the moisture from deep in the ground. Feel the solidity of the roots and trunk. Be aware of the gentle breeze flowing over your branches and leaves, drawing away the unwanted gases and moisture of transpiration. Experience the miracle of photosynthesis as the sunlight warms and energizes your leaves.

There is an aura of Life about you encompassing the whole of the tree. Animals, birds and insects are a part of that life. See them within the soil, the bark, leaves and all around you - a wonderful partnership of sharing, a symbiosis of life stemming from you, the central figure of this place.

Look out over the surrounding land or over the escarpment panorama. All of life is before you, set out in a multitudinous mix or ménage of nature and man managed land.

As you draw a strength and sense of great peace about you, you notice a younger version of yourself approaching the tree, but in some kind of pain or bad mental space. The younger 'you' sits down with his or her back to the tree and draws comfort from that place. As the tree, lean over and let your aura enfold the younger 'you', giving comfort and peace, solace to a troubled soul. Possibly rock the younger 'you' to sleep by the hypnotic sway of your branches and gentle movement of the trunk.

In time, allow the younger 'you' to awaken and leave the tree, restored in some undefined way, for you have helped the younger 'you' in ways beyond your understanding.

When all is quiet, slowly withdraw your consciousness from the tips of the leaves and the roots until you are once again in the trunk at ground level. Step out of the tree, give your greatest thanks and respect to the tree, slowly walk back to the pathway and leave the meadow. Thank your animal friend for guarding you and walk back along the path towards your normal physical life. Leave that place. Return to the here and now, and in your own time open your eyes."

Once again, the symbols not only work their way upon the subconscious, but also describe the individual's state of mind, all without the need to think ahead. So the type of tree, its condition and situation will be indicative of the individual, their desires and imagined emotional state of health. The animal will describe the protective ploys used against the intrusive world as well as providing a sense of safety or protection as the exercise is employed. The landscape will indicate the wider dreams and wishes of the individual, the resources of fantasy that can reflect the deeper resonance with real life. Moreover, of course, the younger version of the individual will indicate a most painful or needy time, sometimes forgotten from conscious memory, but held in pain for years at a time. Here the subconscious throws it up straight away for release and nurture. If it is there, it just happens!

Magical Use

This position is in itself magical. The aim of achieving At-onement is the aim of every magician; however, it is not the monopoly of any magical group or single religious community. The desired experience is to be 'at one' with all creation and appreciate the connectedness of it all. It is also to be aware that the Creator is at the heart of spirituality. This is the basic drive for aspiring magicians. In fact, to be 'At One' is, by definition, holding all things in balance – the Divine, self, creation, others. It must be the aim of every maturing individual to bring balance to their Life, for each and every situation.

To practice either of the previous two exercises will help build an awareness of that connectedness in all creation. Subtle relationships will begin to be appreciated and one's immediate environment will take on a far fuller dynamism, previously undreamt of. To participate knowingly in the complex dance of life is a privilege and responsibility that most people will never know. What a waste!

The other major magical aspect of this position concerns the ability to travel outside the confines of the physical body. If the psychic talent is not present then no amount of exercising is going to generate it. The imagination may be working full blast as the person follows the visualization, but the fantasy remains nothing more than pure self-indulgence. However, if a talent *is* present then regular exercise *will* develop the psychic muscle and fantasy gradually metamorphoses into a truth of subtle signals. For this position of At'Onement the talent under scrutiny is that of astral traveling.

Astral traveling is the ability for the body to remain undisturbed and at rest whilst the mind seems to leave the body confines to wander at will to any part of the physical world [or beyond] or even to mystical realms of the heavens. Whether this is just a way for the mind to assimilate the information as a virtual journey or whether it is in fact a leaving of the body in some way, joined to it by a 'golden chord' like an umbilical link whilst the physical body slumbers, is not the debate at this time. The exercise is one to explore the potential no matter what the explanation. I will leave *that* to the parapsychologists, mystics and weirdoes of this world.

Like most of the 'Magical Uses' that the Qabalah is employed for, the setting is all-important. The setting sets the mind to a certain 'gear' or mode of operation, working to produce results along particular expectations. It is not itself the desired goal but just the means to the end. To find a comfortable and meaningful setting is often the key to success, so I suggest using the archetypal temple but with a futon or suitable bedding at its center. In that way the protection is assured, as well as the undisturbed and private nature of the exercise. The fact that the temple has been employed at the first position does not detract from its usage here. The basic setting is the same but the tools are quite different, so expect a different result.

"Close your eyes and within the privacy of your inner world find yourself standing in the center of a perfect cubed room. There are no doors or windows, just plane surfaces. The walls and ceiling are white, whilst the floor is a patchwork of black and white tiles. Towards one wall is an altar made up of two cubes, one black and the other white. A flame rests within a bowl upon the center of the altar. On either side of the altar stands a column or pillar, representing the feminine and masculine attributes or the yin and yang of all creation, the duality always present. You stand within your magical temple once more. Stand there and decide where you wish to journey as an astral being.

Now create the circle around you, and possibly the pentacle or pentagram within it if you desire, replacing the black and white tiles within the circle with an overall white background to the design. Create some bedding or a futon at its center with the head towards the altar. Place lighted candles at the cardinal points, if you feel it appropriate. Lie down, steady your breathing and heart rate and prepare to leave your body.

Now in your mind's eye, see and feel yourself splitting a duplicate 'you' above and away from your recumbent body. Move your consciousness into the new body and float there for a while, looking down at yourself safe within the temple circle, and joined by a silver or golden chord between the two of you.

Let the Temple dim and the world turn grey as a void or mistiness develops. Then, after a few moments as the mist gradually clears, discover yourself floating above the place you wished to visit. Move in closer and let the detail sharpen. Travel to where you will, free to go without danger and hindrance. Take as long as you wish to discover whatever you wanted or desired. Then, when you are ready, close your 'inner eyes' by dimming the vision or 'greying' it out, and will yourself back to the Temple.

This time, as the vision gradually clears, find yourself whole and reunited with the recumbent 'self', looking around at the temple walls.

In due time stand, let the futon or bedding vanish, stand at the center, let the whole image gradually shimmer and fade, return to the here and now, and in your own time open your eyes."

The exercise can be considered a form of divination or 'forth-telling' in that you may find out what is happening at a distant location without physically traveling there. It may be that something of your soul's essence actually travels to that place, which in turn may be seen by a clairvoyant. Who knows? It does not really matter what the explanation is if the truth of a viewing can be verified. It is a very well documented phenomena and true gift which you may have, but unless you try the exercise regularly for a while and confirm your findings in some way, you may never realize you have it!

Just as for the 'Weather Queen' or 'River of Life', any potential for growth, be it psychical, magical or emotional, can be actualized by regular use. But of course, if a potential is not present, no amount of exercise will develop one.

Only from such a point of balance can true perspective on life be attained; one's strengths, weaknesses, resources and vision. This is just as essential to the magician as to the priest; just as pertinent to the politician as to the parent; just as revealing to the teacher as to the student. It is everyone's magical goal.

Legend, Myth and Religious Comparisons

The Jewish mystical tradition calls this position Tiphereth, which is best understood as Beauty, Harmony and Perfect Balance. Like most of this tradition, the subtlety of meaning is now hopelessly lost. Most commentators fudge the issue and write copiously with high-sounding words, but upon inspection, any interpretation of their work is usually equally mystifying. As far as I can understand this symbolic sphere, the nature of God depicted here somehow contains all elements of the Godhead. The coming manifestation or revelation of God must be present. Also present is the sublime balance of transcendence and yet imminence. There is activity and stillness. There is giving and nurturing to the point of sacrifice and also a demand of response in adoration and service. The Jewish scriptures use the Suffering Servant, the Omnipotent King, the Great Shepherd and the Bridegroom or Husband, with equal force of meaning - and remember these were written long before the New Testament equivalents. This Sephirah holds them all.

Astrologically speaking, the 'planet' that must be the correspondence here is the Sun [no planet at all astronomically speaking but a star] that can nurture *or* burn, however it is the planet of the Ruler, the planet that portrays the individual to the world, the planet of conscious ability, leadership and projection. The Sun can be completely egotistical and self centered to the point of pure selfishness and conceit, but it can also speak of the devotion and sacrifice of a truly great leader, totally dedicated to help, guide and nurture his or her people.

In other religious myth and legend, the Egyptian Ra or Greek Helios, Hyperion, Leo or Apollo all fit the mould. It is a universal symbol of Life, Light and enlightenment. It provides a fertile ground for devolvement to lesser gods and goddesses that encapsulate the ultimate non-judgmental love of sacrifice and new life. Stories of Osiris, Isis and Horus or the Phoenix or, of course, the Death and Resurrection of Jesus, rest most comfortably as correspondences.

The tarot card I have chosen is most certainly not the usual one associated for this position, but with the previous exercise as its evocation, to my way of thinking I believe there can be no other substitute than the Lovers. In the more usual understanding of this card, the Lovers displayed within a layout reflect upon the individual's love life, his or her relationships with the opposite sex. In this instance, the card is elevated to a higher understanding of a cosmic significance or a spiritual maturity. Relationship takes on a far grander stature and interpretation that has ramifications throughout an individual's sense of Relating to the world, which demands a mirroring in the mundane.

The animal I have chosen is the Lion or Stag, both representing the King or Aristocratic Ruler of their empire.

Needless to say, the central position corresponds ideally with the Hero. So Arthur, Robin Hood, Neo [of Matrix fame] or a Viking or Samurai Hero who altruistically fits the bill, is a perfect correspondence. There is no need to explain further, for the Hero is the archetype at the center of all sagas, epics or great tales, the one who all identify with and aspire to – the one who has 'got there'!

The Christian correspondence is Jesus born in Bethlehem – of course. Here is not only the perfect Man – the Son of Man or the Son of God – but Atonement through Christ. I am not trying to proselytize or get one over in an underhand way, but merely present an ironic reflection in that, probably unwittingly, the Christian church [or more fundamentally the Christian tradition] provides the spiritual way of Atonement through identification with Jesus. The Church may speak of "putting one's faith in Christ" or "the Spirit of Christ – the Holy Spirit – coming upon you", but by such identification with the Son of Man the exercise may be much more a prayerful surrender to the hand of God than most people dare dream, and many a professing Christian believer actually experience!!

iv. The Will - Judgment

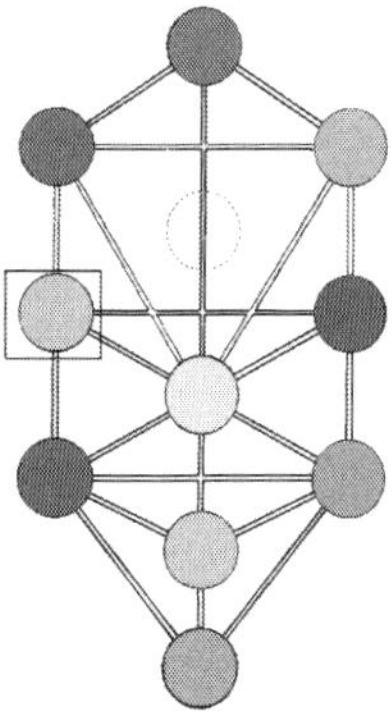

As we move up the Qabalah we begin to see just how interconnected the whole is. Every position has its tension with all other positions. All positions are therefore influenced by, and influence, all the others. The subconscious is one, and although the separate aspects of the mind can be rightly considered as having some kind of intrinsic identity, they really cannot ever be considered to stand on their own in a vacuum. That truly becomes apparent at this level, even if it has not become so already.

At first sight this level might seem to be a contradiction in terms. In the first chapters I pointed out that the language of the subconscious was that of feelings and symbols but the language of the conscious mind was words. The conscious mind was the place for logic and belief systems but motivation originated with the feelings of the subconscious. Justification and rationalization follow on consciously. Therefore, to speak of a rational level within the subconscious seems out of place. However, I am not referring to the logical thought processes of the conscious mind but the way rational thinking might appear to be automatic or instinctive. That truly does belong to the subconscious. I am not splitting hairs for I will speak further of this in a moment.

Just as the position of the 'emotional feminine' for a man might arouse anxiety or wariness when contemplating that concept, so the position of 'rational masculine' might do the same for a woman. There has been more discussed these last few decades over the changing roles of men and women and how society has changed as a result, than ever I can elude to in a paragraph or two. However, I must stress repeatedly that it is not a matter of gender within the Qabalah, but a matter of attribute. This position of rational masculine, which is 'Assessment, Justice in Action', can [and must] be found in both men and women.

One current example of this is how leadership has given ground to consensus. It is a feminine principle to ensure that all voices are heard and considered; it is a masculine principle to take direct control; and in today's western world the committee rules supreme. Perhaps it is because people do not want to take responsibility, for responsibility brings the corresponding risk associated with the 'compensation culture'. However, the once traditional role of male leadership is so eroded that 'the boss' is now generally considered a dinosaur. Whatever the reason may be, this aspect of human experience is in the decline.

Leadership, single-mindedness and broad shoulders all fall into this same category. It is all of these, within the act of judgment, or justice with action, which is the fullness of this position – for *everyone*. It is powered by the previous position of the emotional masculine, but tempered with the spiritual masculine [yet to be looked at] and balanced with the rational feminine of mercy opposite.

I wonder why Judgment is always portrayed with solemn dignity along with an over stated sense of occasion. It's as if the actual process of making judgment has to be undertaken with such an air of gravity that you can almost see the robes, wig, and black hat of the Crown Court Judge sitting in the background, about to pontificate on a matter of life and death. I grant that the alternative Jewish names of "Severity" and "Fear" certainly have such connotations, although I shall write further on these names under the 'Legends etc' section, but "Strength" and "Justice" speaks more of powerful judgment rather than a court of law! Judgment is taking place all the time in nearly all types of activity, and most usually without any acknowledgment or fear of 'Judgment' at all!

Consider the situation of making choices. Judgment is undertaken if you have to make the choice between eating a large piece of cake without cream or a small piece of cake with cream. That means, of course, that you have already made the 'serious' decision that you wish to limit the calories, but now you are concerned about how the level of carbohydrate and calorie intake can be kept in check. It is a matter of debating with yourself as how best to work the parameters. Hardly a situation that demands Judge Deed, complete in black hat - or does it?!!! If, in fact, you find it near to impossible to make that kind of decision, then it only goes to show that this exercise is most necessary. But do note that this position is *not* about making any particular decision and the rightness or wrongness of that decision - that is a function of the conscious mind. This exercise is designed to evoke the unconscious competent *ability* to make judgments and decisions - that is the function of the subconscious mind.

Judgment involves the application of knowledge and experience within a presented situation. It is part of the learning curve of ability. Take, for example, the process of learning to drive. At first you probably are not aware of just how ignorant [or incompetent] a driver you are. That is unconscious incompetence. Then quickly you proceed onto conscious incompetence. That is where everything must be most consciously carried out using the pedals, wheel and bits and pieces in order to proceed, albeit erratically to begin with! You have begun to learn. Unconscious incompetence has rapidly made way to conscious incompetence, as the realization dawns as to how much there is to learn about driving a car. Then familiarity with the controls grows. Driving skills improve with practice, until the conscious *incom*petence gives ground to conscious *com*petence, and it becomes an enjoyable experience to drive. *In time,* as the skills improve, then the position becomes that of *un*conscious competence, especially if 'automatic pilot' engages from time to time and you 'awaken' with a start and wonderment as to how you got to that place without an accident! That is subconscious 'rational' thinking. Hopefully the process does not go any further, and familiarity breeds contempt to the point of becoming a bad driver after all!

This exercise is designed to facilitate the application of learnt skills and understanding, and to make judgments continually, but quite unconsciously and competently – Strength and Justice in action.

Self-Awareness

"Close your eyes, and once again let the consciousness move from the possible points of intrusion, to the picture gradually developing in the inner world of the subconscious.

In your mind's eye picture yourself standing upon a cliff top pathway, looking out to sea. Feel the stiff breeze blowing inshore, pushing you with careless gusting shoves backwards towards the land. Notice the ships on the far horizon and the wheeling and diving of the sea birds along the cliff face and shoreline, playing on the updrafts and chasing the waves as they roil and break upon the sand. Imagine what it might be like to be one of them.

Deliberately change your shape, for you make up the rules in this place, and become a bird – known or imaginary – standing on the cliff top. Open your wings and let the breeze lift you and carry you aloft. Tip your wings, fly forwards passing the cliff edge, and so glide high and out from the land. Swoop towards the sea and begin to fly amidst the other birds, enjoying the sheer freedom of flight and speed over the breaking surf. Dart amongst them and twist and turn. "Chase me if you can" is the name of the game, so play it with utter abandon. Delight in your abilities and be at one with the others, the wind and the sea. Play with the spray and play with the wind as it gusts and abates in a never-ending dance with the wave tops. Have a sense of the hidden depths, currents and sheer volume of the sea beneath you. Ride the flow of air and follow it up the cliff face, soaring high many times the height of the cliff, high into the sky.

Glide in a hardly perceptible fall out over the sea towards a ship. Look down upon the humans as they work their passage across the sea, chained by gravity to the surface of their craft, slow in movement and laborious in their work. Fly high above them and pity them for a moment in their relative imprisonment and stodgy toil.

Seek the heights and soar aloft again, a partnership of wings, effort, and then sudden effortless lift – a gift from the wind. Reach higher and higher until the air becomes rarefied, yet find no difficulty in breathing. Reach yet higher again until the sky becomes darker, not dark from a storm but dark from the darkness of space – and then hang there in utter stillness, silence and solitude. The stars seem as diamonds of light in the violet sky all around, and the brightness of sea and activity far below can be watched and understood as a mystery of life, accepted as part of what is and what should be. A wonderful panorama holding the completeness of life, that only needs a closer look to gain detail and knowledge of whatever you want just by turning your attention upon it. Rest there for a while and exult in the ecstasy of privilege.

Begin to return to earth, slowly falling through the air. Let the ground come up to greet you. Spot your initial point of leaving the cliff and gradually glide in to land. Stand and look out to sea once again and change back into a human once more.

With the feeling of work well done in your being, gently let that scene shimmer and die, return to the here and now, and in your own time open your eyes".

The Air is the corresponding element of the mind, and the exercise places you deep within it, above the sea of emotion with all its currents, hidden depths and vastness. That does not mean there is an absence of emotion - far from it. The exercise shows you can 'play' with it, be friends with it, and rejoice with it, acknowledge its strength, depth and breadth, but it also shows that it does not have to control you in all things. You rise above it and see it in its place.

The way you delight with your ability to fly evokes the urge to delight in mental play, judging how to work towards the desired result, and automatically adjusting your 'wings' to achieve that. Your skill is only limited by your imagination. You are evoking that automatic judgment of working with confidence. You can 'rise' to great heights and, from the elevated position, gain insight in whatever area you want. It is all a matter of perspective, knowledge, and understanding of limits and abilities – Judgment.

As that is the case, the way the symbols present themselves show your ability, desire or dearth of judgment. By now you can surely interpret them for yourself, and be your best judge of where you are and what you need to develop.

Therapeutic Involvement

At the emotional level of the Qabalah, it is easily recognized how the therapeutic involvement is primarily working upon the emotions of the individual. What is far harder to appreciate is how the therapeutic involvement works at the rational/mental level. Obviously RET [Rational Emotive Therapy] and NLP [Neuro-linguistic Programming] and CBT [Cognitive Behavioral Therapy] have their place here, but they stand within their own therapy protocols. An exercise that endeavors to incorporate the principles from these can be devised, but it can only be a template that needs the particular situation parameters to be included. The setting of an exercise accesses this part of the subconscious, but the real-life situation requirements must refine the central imagery. Let me give you an example of this such as encouraging self-worth or confidence. It is an exercise that simply makes use of the visualization of the skeleton, yet the implications are staggering. The setting for this exercise is based on the Castlerigg circle of stones in the Lake District.

"Open your mental eyes and find yourself climbing upwards along a path towards a circle of stones, positioned high on a moor land fell. The stones form quite a large circle and all are present – there are no gaps in the circle. The ground is flat and dry, perched on a level shelf of the fell. It is early in the day and the air is crystal clear. The sun is just rising and no one is around.

Approach the circle and stand in a gap to prepare yourself for the work ahead. You are here to ask for more confidence and the ability to stand up for your beliefs and opinions. Take off your shoes - or more if you feel it appropriate – and, when you are ready, slowly enter the circle and stand at its center. Face the dawn sun on the far horizon.

Just as for the Weather Queen, but nowhere to the same degree as for that exercise [!], be aware of power rising from the depths of the ground, winding around as a spiral, to enter the circle at your feet.

Be aware of the feet slightly apart – not as a collection of many bones, but as two solid units of the body giving stability to the whole, very grounded and very secure. It is like being anchored to the ground, rooted to the earth. So be aware of a deeper inner stance to life - that of being secure and grounded, no matter what life may throw at you.

The energy enters the legs, so be aware of them, possibly longer, straighter, slender, but very firm. Such a stance brings a greater viewpoint, higher and more far reaching, linking that stability of the grounded feet to the rest of the body. There is also realized a potential for locomotion, easy far reaching strides to get to where you want go. A person's thinking cannot remain static. There needs to be an appreciation of mental vision and a willingness to venture far in thought.

The energy continues to climb up the body and enters the abdomen. Hold the pelvis in mind as a large bowl containing the vital organs of the body, safe, guarded and secure behind their walls of strong and most solid bone. Your vulnerability is closely guarded, your innermost secrets safe and secure.

The energy rises and the spine straightens and elongates. It is like a metal rod of support, enabling the ribs to expand and the lungs to take in more life giving air. Your 'backbone' is stronger; giving it added strength to bear up against life's brickbats. Your shoulders are wider and more able to carry a load. It is amazing just how much responsibility, strain and stress you can, in fact, take.

The energy travels along the bones of your arms and hands. They can be seen as strong, supple, dexterous manipulators and tools of the body. Not only do we live in the world, but also we work our will upon it. We can delight in our control of all around us, lords of all creation.

Once more the energy rises and now it enters the head. The skull – the very symbol of life and death - is the crowning piece, giving clear aspect to the world around, protecting the most mysterious brain and place of self or ego. The crown gives a sense of worth, of royalty even, and of presence and knowing. You stand there at the center of the circle, with regal bearing.

Be aware of the whole body. The grounded feet, the firm but striding legs, the guardian pelvis, the strong backbone, the dexterous arms, the high crown skull - all can be held in mind for a while in that place, alive and alert, looking out at the world shown beyond and below the circle. You are ready to face the new day with all that that might bring.

In due time let the energy ebb away, relax and so move back to the gap in the stones from which you entered this place of work. Dress if necessary – make a gesture of respect – turn, and leave that place. As you walk back along the path, let that image shimmer and fade, return to the here and now, and in your own time open your eyes."

The setting, which is an equivalent of the Magical Temple in the first position of the Qabalah, prepares you for the work. Here though, it is firmly acknowledged to be a work of the mind, an act of will, even though the connections are symbolized and implicit with the physical and emotional parts of your being.

The actual therapeutic work is the work upon your 'inner' body, changing it, if necessary, to be more stable, strong, guarded, flexible and sure. The outcome cannot be a physical change in your body, except by change of stance and posture, but the change of mental stance assumed in the exercise, should bring about change at the deeper level of unconscious competence, that is the desired result. The grounded feet should bring a greater sense of 'feet on the ground' approach to life, a more stable outlook and a surety of 'where you are', and so on.

Different systems of the body can be used as the inner workings, to evoke different responses. So the energetic system brings an increase of awareness with the energetic world in which we live and evokes an energetic response within us; the circulatory system increases awareness of the connectedness of life and the way the heart, or love, is the binding force of all; the energetic air or prana breathed in, brings an 'a-livening' and uplifting of the spirit; the lymphatic and immune system strengthens the sense of being protected from the ills of this world and the ability to see death as part of life. This list is not comprehensive at all. The imagery can be tailored to suit the circumstances that are presented, and the way to counter the challenge from within.

Not to be forgotten are the consequences of any action - of whatever kind. Any action demands a reaction of some kind or other. In the case of healing, the unexpected reaction may go against the very thing you think is needful. You may want to ease suffering but the end result may be worse that the initial state. It is sometimes an act of kindness to let a person die or to suffer, in order to gain perspective or understanding. Remember that it may be that you have to go through hell or physical torment in order to spiritually grow. The scales of justice can represent Action and Reaction just as easily as a considered debate or judgment, so be careful what you 'pray' for. You might just get it!

We cannot really forget that Mercy and Compassion, the next Qabalah position, have a part to play in all healing work. The effect that Compassion has will depend upon the ethical stance, as well as the integrity of the healer. Someone may see abortion as the necessary or 'best of the worst' choices, while another person might only see that as complete anathema. However, the exercise and work is not about the forming of a moral framework for that belongs to the conscious mind. It is about being empowered to make judgment and subsequently work accordingly.

Magical Use

The magical use is so close to the therapeutic exercise that there is no need to repeat the visualization. This position is ideal for absent healing and, as such, could surely be alternatively named 'The Healer'. You can either imagine the patient being the person in the center of the circle, receiving the healing as you see it, or you can still be the person at the center, healing them as they stand, kneel or lie before you. You bring the person, for whom you work the magic, to the desired place when you are ready and, by placing your hands upon them or not [personal inclination and choice], change them or give them the power to change themselves.

Magic can be sought and worked at nearly all of the positions, but to be most efficacious, the differing positions of the Qabalah reflect the differing *kinds* of magical work that might be best placed more formally within that particular position and setting. In that case, of course, as this is the position of working the will, it could just as easily be thought of as the magician's place. However, I consider the Weather Queen as *the* magician's place, the place for cursing or blessing, bringing death or giving life – a place of POWER. Here is a place of WORK, which takes place within quietness and a settled air of determination. I acknowledge that this position might be the place of sending 'change' from afar, but I much prefer to emphasize the healer rather than the magician here, and leave the magician firmly at the emotional level.

The stone circle is a traditional place of magic as well as worship, but more thought of in the way of working with nature, especially that of health and fecundity. As magic is the bringing about of change by the application of will, so the setting cannot be bettered with respect to correspondences for the Celt. Even the Magical Temple of the first position is artificial, in the sense that that image lacks the natural connectedness to the world, whereas this imagery has a connectedness inbuilt from the start. Conversely, there is also a sense of detachment, giving space to think rather than react, a height of perspective and an outlook of respect, rather than instant involvement and confrontational change! It may lack the power of the Weather Queen, but it brings a thoughtful perspective that might just be a better choice of venue that a particular situation really requires.

Legend, Myth and Religious Comparisons

Noting that I have switched the two Sephiroth at this level, the Jewish mystical tradition calls this position Geburah, which is best understood as Justice, Severity, and Fear. Let me remind you that it just seems to be the traditional place for Geburah, but as I have switched the pillars around so I have also switched the individual Sephiroth at this level, maintaining the family of attributes.

A practicing Jew will tell you that the obvious consequence of translation is quite incorrect. It is not a matter of fear, standing as an emotion in its own right, which all people experience from time to time. It is a matter of a living relationship with the Divine Creator and Upholder of his people. Although the Jew might go in fear and trembling of God, God is also the God of Love – the shepherd of his sheep. The sense is thus one of awe and overwhelming *respect,* to ever be in the mind or presence of the Divine. It is not the cringing abject fear in this case, but the sense of 'one's place' against that of the Almighty. As we shall see when we look at the balancing position of Chesed, the Severity or Awesomeness of God is balanced with the Mercy and Love of God – the two cannot be divorced from each other – ever. Fear is not that which comes from severity of judgment experienced as pain and suffering, but respect and loving obedience to the greatness of God.

Quickly changing the religious framework - the Egyptian symbols of the crook and the flail come to mind, for one was never present without the other. If one was lifted, the other was also taken in hand *at the same time* – never were the two separated whilst in the presence of Pharaoh.

Astrologically speaking, the 'planet' that is usually placed here is Mars, symbolizing strength and severity more than fear; however, I have already said that I prefer to see that particular planet positioned at the emotional level of the Weather Queen, representing the masculine emotional power. The planet

Mercury seems to fit better here in my opinion, for here is more the quiet and rational or thinking position, considering all consequences before action. The Egyptian god Thoth, the equivalent Greek Hermes and the Roman Mercury most aptly describe the healer divinity, wise in action and steeped in experience and skill.

The Tarot card I have placed here is the Emperor, for he has to be most able in all his judgments if ever he is to survive and rule well. His people depend upon him just for continued life, prosperity, and good peaceful government. He is not acting from a remote height, but an informed and intelligent closeness or involvement in the world. He is the closest image in the tarot to the Jewish God of loving judgment.

The animal that fits my ideal at this point is the Wolf – and not a bird of the self-awareness exercise! Certainly not the wildness of the Bull that Mars would demand, but a cunning, swift and most able masculine hunter, with an air of aristocracy that is missing in the Fox, for example.

The Christian tradition does not easily fit at this point. It lacks a personality and presence, unlike the Jewish tradition. I believe simply placing the balancing 'Word' with the next position of 'Sacrament' goes some way to representing the necessary correspondence. It introduces the thinking person who needs to interpret the scriptures, before acting upon them. It has a scholastic inference that acknowledges the untold debate of the centuries and strength of endurance and survival that the ravages of ignorant destruction and the Dark Ages could not overcome. It also presents the deeper understanding of "the Word going Forth". The Word is, therefore, the magic of God at work, either in evangelism or miracle working. The priesthood works its own form of magic in the exercise of prayer. So the biblical understanding of 'the Word' is not a static, dry and academic understanding, rather it is a dynamic phenomenon, in that the Word once spoken has an effect. The gospel is spoken and demands a reaction – that is evangelism. The prayer or command must be answered or obeyed. The Word went forth over the waters and Creation took place.

The correspondences in myth and legends are far less obvious, reflecting the deepening difficulty of placing something here. The KeyMaker might best represent the modern Matrix personality, while in the Arthurian legend, Lancelot might be the one placed here - although I think it is pushing things. Possibly Little John stands within the Robin Hood system, but certainly it is much harder for the imagination to find a person that obviously fits the bill. Quite a reversal from the more usual situation!

vii. Mercy - Compassion and Forgiveness

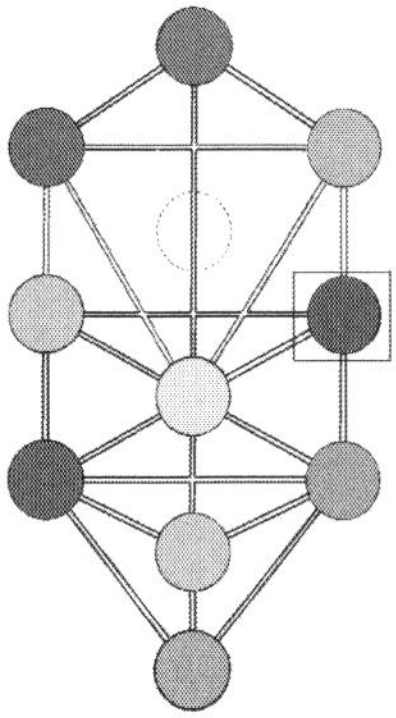

The 'higher' up the Qabalah you investigate, the harder it is to truly accept the response. Self-awareness is *absolutely essential* at these levels, for the lower levels are almost self-explanatory and little in the way of avoidance is instigated for those who fear to accept the unpalatable truth of self-examination. That is not the case at the 'higher' levels. At these positions *absolute honesty* is crucial, especially at this position, yet repeatedly you find avoidance and justification of the issues. We all like to think we are more ethical, mature and spiritual than in fact we probably are.

Restating the obvious - the whole of the feminine column balances that of the masculine column, and the more we progress into the Qabalah the more we see how the Qabalah acts as a whole - every position being in tension with all the others. We have already seen how the position of rational masculine 'Judgment' is powered by the masculine 'Weather Queen', and retains integrity by the yet to be explored position of masculine 'Wisdom'. It is also balanced by this rational feminine position of 'Mercy', for without it 'Judgment' becomes the despot or tyrant. In similar vein, 'Mercy' is powered by the position of 'Being and Feeling', especially with relation to the more needy 'Pain and Suffering'. It is inspired by the yet to be explored 'Intuition', and, of course, balanced by the previous position of 'Judgment'. Without that balance 'Mercy' becomes capricious or simply empty and meaningless.

I must stress that this is a rational level position, for in many people's opinion Compassion and Mercy are thought more of as emotions stemming from a reactive stimulus, rather than a rational thought out stance and process. However, judgment occurs in the everyday situation as a 'subconscious or unconscious competence' process that has arisen from the learning curve of growing ability, knowledge and experience. In the same way, 'Compassion and Mercy' is a similar process. They stem from a developed stance to appear in actual situations as an automatic or reactive 'emotion'.

It is so easy to confuse this point so let me put it in another way. Judgment involves an *assessment* that is put into action in some way or other. Likewise Mercy, the developed ethical and compassionate stance, cannot be just an intellectual concept existing in a vacuum. It involves a *previous thought out process* and action of some kind along the spectrum of acceptance and tolerance through to forgiveness or an actual act of charity, even though it might be so swift a process to seem as an instinctive emotion.

Notice, it was not the rightness or wrongness of any judgment that was being assessed at the last position, but the ability to *process* judgment. So neither is it the degree of goodness or badness associated with mercy, but the dispensation or lack of doing so that is in highlighted here.

The belief systems that involve rightness or wrongness, and goodness or badness, belong to the conscious mind and rational thought out framework of belief. The process of implementation of both Judgment and Mercy works [or does not work!] at the subconscious depths of the mind. Remember, the Qabalah is not really about conscious processes of the mind, but about subconscious, seemingly instinctive ones.

Possibly the best professional or clinical appreciation of this position is to regard the difference between empathy and sympathy. Sympathy is where the prevailing emotion stems from one's own experience and is projected upon the presenting situation. Empathy is the sought after 'getting alongside' the other person's emotional state, trying to understand it and get a feel of its strength and direction. Thus sympathy is derived more from the lower levels of both masculine and feminine emotion stemming from one's own past memories, while empathy is that rational process of identifying with the other person to gain understanding and insight. In fact psychiatric Professor James Harris, of John Hopkins University USA, goes further to describe Compassion as being when a person *acts* on *empathy*.

Perhaps a mundane example, more on a par with the judgment concerning pieces of cake, is of a parent coping with the unruly child. The parent must surely be affected by a child's emotional tantrum or outburst. There are too many stories of such constant emotional battering, leading to the snapping of self control and a violent response against the child. A parent cannot be Superman or Wonder Woman all the time, yet life often demands exactly that. To make instant choices of judgment, that also show compassion and love to the child [and to self!], is the ability that is being worked upon or evoked here - *not* the wisdom of choice or the rightness or wrongness of any single action. Rather, it is trying to understand the situation from the child's point of view, and balance the care with judgment. In that case, how is it best to teach, love and care for the child, within the tolerance, emotional reserves and ability of the parent, at that time?

A more acute example of the process of compassion is when a person justifies an action rather than owning up to an inadequacy, especially if the justification hides behind a religious or philosophical doctrine or dogma. The 'Turn the Other Cheek' ploy is so well worn that it is hardly ever questioned by onlookers. Rather it is more likely to be applauded or respected! Take the following as an example:-

Suppose a mature citizen – a priest - was walking along a

street when he encountered a group of youths. Due to the unexpected nature of the encounter he was unprepared for trouble, and upon demands for money and credit cards, meekly handed them over. Later, being questioned by the authorities, he explained his actions as a putting into practice his religious beliefs, i.e. he 'turned the other cheek'. Although, of course, that *could* well be the real reason, it is much more likely that the cheek was turned for him! In other words he didn't stand a snowball's chance in hell of getting away with anything else. In this case, the situation was judged that survival meant compliance. His emotions would have probably included anger, fear and utter helpless frustration or rage, but in order to survive they would have been controlled or even smothered and later actually denied – even to himself. That constitutes a lying justification, for in reality he had no choice in the matter.

On the other hand, if a black-belt, fourth Dan, karate expert encountered the same group, and endured the same demands for cash and credit cards, he might very well do the very same thing and hand them over. Of course he might not! But, assuming he did, then his statement to the authorities would probably have been the very same. His deeper reasoning undoubtedly would have been quite different, but to any onlooker the two situations would have been identical. However, I can see that in the second situation the karate expert could very easily have fought off any attack by the group and retained his cash and cards. In this second instance he deliberately 'turned the other cheek' - it was not turned for him – and his emotions would have been tempered by his previously thought out ethical stance and motivation. An instinctual awareness of danger would have been present, but this would *not* have been the overwhelming primarily emotion as experienced by the priest. In all probability, in this hypothetical situation, he had some degree of compassion and pity for the young men. Because of his ability to easily fight them off, he had the space to see their paucity of spirit. It is not up to us to condone his action or necessarily agree with it, but just to look on and understand it. His desire to help would have gone into his decision making, along with his judgment of ability and experience in coping with aggression. He decided not to meet aggression with aggression. This is 'unconscious competent mercy'!

This position is *not* a duplication of the lower emotional level. It is *not* seeing the reactive choice or reality in its fullness and being able to make a choice constrained within that. It is somehow creating greater choice, and *immediate choice,* from a past thoughtful perspective and from greater personal integrity. *It is also not a position to examine or evaluate a moral framework or ethical stance itself. That mental activity belongs to the conscious mind.*

This exercise, like that of the rational masculine position, is also designed to facilitate the application of learnt skills and understanding, and to implement decision making along the lines of compassion and mercy, but quite unconsciously and competently. I have used the ethical symbols of 'castles, woodland and magic' in a fantasy world setting.

Self-Awareness

"Close your eyes, and once again let the consciousness move from the possible points of intrusion to the picture gradually developing in the inner world of the subconscious. The inner world, this time, is of an unexpected fantasy nature involving mythical beasts and magical implements.

In your mind's eye picture yourself walking through a primeval forest in the semi-darkness. You are dressed as a person of power - a mage, witch, wizard, or sorcerer - for that is what you truly are, with a cloak or habit with cowl, a satchel and staff. You are on a mission through dangerous lands to procure a talisman of power that will restore your daughter to consciousness and life. It is a small, weighty object, yet its shape really cannot be discerned, for it is a thing of light. It fits nicely in the hand, but to carry it you covered it with velvet cloth and placed it in your satchel. It will only work for a single magic and you are afraid that if you keep holding it you might inadvertently use it. Then your journey will be wasted - with tragic consequences. Without it she will surely die, for she ate of a poison that has no remedy, except that that belongs in the magical realm. You have journeyed for several days and are deadly tired. You have obtained the talisman at considerable cost and energy – and are now so close to returning to your fortress home and castle with your precious load.

You enter a clearing along your path and stop to clear your head, wipe your brow and ease the stitch in your side. To give you room to stretch, you place your staff on the ground and bend your back in a circular movement. As you bend forwards you receive a tremendous whack on your back that almost, but not quite, knocks you to the ground, with bewildering and exquisite pain.

You turn and see an ogre standing a few yards behind you, intent upon repeating the attack. You are obviously his intended next meal, so make your defense as quickly as you can. Your tiredness has let you down, and your guard, so assiduously kept until now, has been lost. Now, although you raise your arms for a spell of binding, you know deep down that it has little power in your exhausted state, unless you use your staff as the magic wand that it truly is. There is little hope of that, for by the time you looked and reached for the staff on the ground you would lose what little advantage of time you had. The ogre could close the distance between you and give you the final reckoning, a blow that would land you in the next world of spiritual advancement, satisfying his appetite in the bargain! You are helpless and despair sets in. You are at his mercy!

You just look at him, as he looks at you. You have always under-

stood that ogres are dim-witted and perpetually hungry. He is massive and looks well fed – no wonder, for his prey could have little chance against such strength, reach and primitive power.

The seconds extend into minutes, but still he does not make his move. You kick yourself for your careless lapse, but self-recrimination cannot save the day. You can almost cry out in despair, for it is not only your life that is forfeit due to your folly.

It gradually dawns upon you that he is observing you, your powerlessness and empty threat. He knows your tiredness is his greatest advantage and yet he does nothing against you. He knows he has you in his grasp. He knows there is nothing you can really do, and yet still he just stands there and looks at you.

With amazement on your part, you stand open mouthed as he smiles at you, drops his attacking stance and turns and walks away! He has let you go – for whatever reason. How can you know the mind of an ogre? He has shown you mercy and spared your life. You just accept your great fortune, quickly take up your staff and continue on your journey.

After a distance you spy your home and castle ahead on the path. It is set within a cliff-face across a gorge of unfathomed depth. As you approach you can see that the drawbridge is down awaiting your return, for no moment can be lost to bring the life-giving remedy to your one and only daughter. Even the great door is open and a servant awaits you at the entrance. You pull the satchel around and with your free hand search within it to locate and unfold the talisman from its protective custody. You hold it ready and glowing for instant administration to bring that miracle and magical remedy.

As you step onto the bridge once again there is an attack, for a rock is thrown from behind and hits you in the middle of your back. It is clear the ogre did not intend to leave you alone, or possibly he changed his mind. Stumbling very badly, you drop your staff and stagger forwards from the impact. You stumble towards the drawbridge side and desperately try to regain your balance. Clutching at air, you tumble over the edge into the emptiness of the bottomless chasm.

You have only seconds in which to act. Your choices are limited and you can only attempt once whatever you choose to do.

- *There is power in the talisman to retaliate and kill the ogre, as you fall to your death;*
- *you can throw the talisman to the waiting servant and hope that he will catch it and be able to close the door before the ogre charges the drawbridge and you fall to your death;*
- *you can cast a spell of levitation, float away from the confrontation or regain the drawbridge and momentary safety, but lose all chance of saving your daughter;*
- *you can blast the drawbridge to smithereens, but condemn all within it to a lingering death of starvation, for there is only the one way in or out to home and castle.*

The choice is yours. IMMEDIATELY make your choice NOW, for the scene shimmers and fades and you return to the here and now.

No one needs know what you attempted, or why, or if you were unable to act. In your own time open your eyes."

Just as before with the position of Masculine Rational, the purpose is to evoke the unconscious competence associated with this level. What is not being sought here is the ability to make a judgment between the various alternatives presented in the exercise, but to understand the motivation behind your choice and develop that sense of mercy to temper the judgment. Most situations in Life do not allow us the luxury of debate but demand an immediate response to the presented scenario. Therefore, in all probability, a person following the exercise is immediately on the defensive and prepared to justify their choice.

That is not the point of the exercise. It is not about the rightness or wrongness of any choice, but the degree of mercy involved, to whom it is shown and where within you the need to show mercy arose. Mercy colors all our decision making, even though we might deny such. Yet it is not the motivation stemming from a religious persuasion being sought here, for that comes from a higher position and experience. It is the awareness that the spectrum of Mercy and Forgiveness exists within you, and how strong the automatic application and strength of this. Where it is derived from, i.e. the spectrum of simply guilt or push-button emotional reaction through to deep spiritual integrity, tells us whether this position is weak and needs working upon, or whether the influence of Mercy is already operating at a subconscious competence level and degree.

The first alternative could be seen just as an emotional response of vengeance. You have failed in your quest and someone else has to pay! It could also be an endeavor to save the innocent bystanders in the situation. Why should the servant or servants die because of you and your daughter's folly? Are your lives more important than theirs?

The second alternative hangs onto the last vestige of hope for your daughter's recovery for there is still risk from the ogre. Does this show mercy for your daughter or a selfish desire to see her well above all other issues? Do you believe in 'Life after Death' and not see that you will be reunited in moments?

The third alternative could be seen as either a most selfish act on your part, yet it could be a way of making amends by thereafter living a life of selfless devotion to teach others of the ways of magic and healing. Also you could always have another daughter!

The fourth alternative could be a sense of Justice shown towards the servants. You and your daughter, the main players in this scenario, are to die, whilst the ogre is thwarted, but the drawbridge was down and door open because the servant put speed before safety. They also deserve to suffer, but could possibly find a way to cross the chasm if they have the wit and resources.

What your choices were can be explored at leisure, for they show your strength of integrity or emotional reaction, balanced by ability and judgment. The various threads that lead to a particular choice indicate Mercy in action - or the lack of it. They could reveal a cold logical judgment, sense of revenge, or the futility of Life. It is how you honestly see or interpret the action that is the true indicator of how active Mercy, Acceptance and Forgiveness really are and how unconsciously you apply them. We are NOT really deeply interested in the rightness, wrongness, goodness or badness of the choice, except in that they indicate the ability, or lack of it, to allow judgment and mercy to operate!

The greatest sense of honesty is called for here. Others need never know your decision, so you only fool yourself if you cheat! I have repeatedly pointed out that you make the rules in your inner world, but in this case, if you changed the rules and made other alternatives it is more likely to show that you are evading the issue, rather than face the challenge and experience. I put it to you that it is the minority of people who actually *do* work with clarity of Mercy, even at the conscious incompetence level - let alone the conscious competence or especially the subconscious competence level. Most people are only swayed by the emotions of Love, Fear or Self Interest, yet believe that they have a degree of objectivity and decide from an evolved ethical stance. What do your decisions show about you?

The exercise repeated several times, and the changing emotions associated with your decisions, will show your self-awareness or self-deception far better than any words of warning from me can instigate. Be warned though, for it is so, so easy to delude yourself!

Therapeutic Involvement

Last chapter, I pointed out that in the case of healing it is sometimes an act of kindness to let a person die or to suffer in order to gain perspective or understanding for it may be that you have to go through hell or physical torment in order to spiritually grow. The Healer, contained in Judgment, must make room for alternatives to be assessed before any healing is given. It is at this position that the feminine attribute of 'receiving' can be taken quite literally, in that alternatives can be 'received' for your judgment. Of course balance is required, but a course of action is not simply given at the Judgment position without some kind of reference to the consequences. It is the discovery at this position of several alternatives, which widen the understanding of the nature of 'healing'. I suggest that in order to gain appreciation of such alternatives the Circle of Stones of the Healer's Temple might be viewed as multiple variations of a theme!

"In your mind's eye climb the path towards the Circle of Stones, but this time, instead of stopping and working within that circle, pass on by to a higher elevation and look down upon the place of work. See yourself as you work at a particular problem such as that described before, of the evocation of confidence and strength of inner conviction or belief. Now look to one side and see an identical circle with an identical 'you' working just as before, but this time acknowledge there are subtle differences.

Study the two side by side. Identify the differences. Perhaps one shows a more upright or taller you. Perhaps the other shows a more tired or older you, but with brighter, more 'alive' eyes. This position opens up alternatives and the balance means that you must decide which is the most fitting – hopefully unconsciously competently. If you really want to, you can let the reasoning of the choice dawn within your mind, but it is not necessary!

You then return down the path back towards one of the circles of stones – the one you decided is the 'right' one. Move to a gap in the circle preparatory to the healing work, and continue as before.

However, this time you may have a more wholesome version to work to......."

It might be that this time it is more important that you accept a lesser profile or smaller outer image of ego, for a brighter or stronger inner understanding of spiritual place and humility. Healing, on this occasion, becomes the acceptance of constraint of some kind rather than battling against the outer odds - or the other way around. Hopefully, fed by the Intuition from the next level, and held in tension by the emotional need from below, the Healer [Judgment] is moved by the insight gained from the Feminine principle. That is when the various parts of the whole of the subconscious are working 'as an integrated team'!

The two positions of the Rational level, just like for the two on the Emotional level, work together. They feed each other almost in a symbiotic manner. As one is worked, the other benefits - it is mutually reciprocally so.

Magical Use

When we were looking at the Emotional level we saw that the masculine position was essentially one of 'active' or 'doing' in some way, while the feminine position was that of 'passive' or being. Of course there were degrees of activity or passivity, but the essential understanding of the attribute held. Force and Form were both required for the magic to be effective and grow in power. Similarly, at the Rational level we find the same need for balance. Whereas Judgment involved the active 'doing' or dispensing of justice, demanded by any particular situation - the giving out of some kind of understanding, the feminine is 'being' merciful or compassionate and receiving some kind of understanding. Let me explain.

It might have been better for me to have changed my usual format at this position and to first look at the Magical Use before the Therapeutic Use this once, as it might have helped to more easily understand something of the principles at work. For whereas the emphasis at the Emotional level is obviously emotions, and the way they play such a significant part in therapy, so the emphasis at the Rational level is the unconscious competence of the mind and the ability to use that mind in an 'act of Will'. So the Magician and the Healer can be one and the same, especially when both sides of the Rational level are balanced. However, in this instance, rather than sending forth one's Will to work upon a situation or heal a person - the Word going Forth, it is more a receiving of a widened vision or a backdrop to Judgment, which is associated with Feeling or Compassion. To accept, understand and use that widened vision necessitates tools of the trade, so it is my suggestion that at this position of the 'Within' forms of the archetypal symbols can be perceived, appreciated or understood more directly in some way. It cannot be the actual archetypes themselves for that is not possible, but there might well be 'seen' a personification of the archetypes. These could even be represented by the Masters of Magical Lore that present themselves before the magical merciful practitioner to work with. Let me explain further.

Elementals are invoked at the lower levels of the emotions through such exercises as the Weather Queen of deep gut-level energy. Some kind of though form or even Divas, Lords of aspects of creation, are contacted or invoked at this Rational level. Here it is the symbol of the 'group identity' of some aspect of creation that can be sought out, understood and 'used' with respect. It is as if the various choices discovered within the Therapeutic exercise, or the alternative realities that might be desired by the Judgment magician, can somehow be personified and given life!

It is my advice to the magician that before any emphatic working of the Will upon the world is undertaken, that the last therapeutic exercise is employed in a magical way, specifically to seek clarification through personification. The relevant archetype, Diva or Guide might be seen in symbolic form. Even the 'sense of rightness of choice' may present itself as a thought form within the observed circle, to warn or inform you before irrevocable harm or a particular action is taken. Heed the symbols, if ever they come. Learn to accept them, and let them temper or balance the opposite position. Ultimately, though, it is your responsibility and not the consensus of some kind of group mind, Diva or thought form that you can hide behind, for *you* are one who perceives in this way and works your will upon the world.

Legend, Myth and Religious Comparisons

Recalling the switched designation, the Jewish Mystical tradition calls this position Gebulah or more usually Chesed, which is understood best as Mercy, Compassion or even Grace. To my way of thinking, this firmly places it in the family attribute of Feminine Rational. Perhaps this is the best understood nature of the Jewish God by the gentile mind, or perhaps it is because this is the aspect of God most people want to believe in! It is the loving Father or Shepherd of the sheep. Caricaturized and epitomized, it is the kindly old man sitting in splendor on the heavenly throne – the 'everybody's loving uncle' that would not hurt a fly. Undoubtedly this is an aspect of God, but NEVER to be taken on its own or to that extreme degree. Any serious student of the Divine will cringe at that picture - but also accept something of its portrayal.

Astrologically speaking, the planet that is placed here is Jupiter, the Great Benevolent, symbolizing Generosity of Spirit, Acceptance and Joviality. What is rather surprising is that although it is the position of Feminine Rationality, Jupiter or Jove is the King of the gods, a male. That is reminiscent of the Weather Queen at the Masculine Emotional level or the Bull in the feminine Taurus zodiac sign. The attribute is the stressed understanding rather than the logical and neat classification from gender.

The Tarot card I have placed here is the Empress, for she traditionally holds the Emperor's hand and plays the mercy card. It is the loving wife of the ruler that folk lore depicts as having great love for her people and always holds them in her heart - hence the Queen of Hearts, archetypically donned or put upon the late Diana, Princess of Wales. No matter what *her* motivation might have been, the people would not have believed any other kind of motivation could be a possibility. So the Empress is a must!

The Dolphin is the animal that seems to fit best for me. It encapsulates the kindly love that is somehow also difficult to express. It is felt rather than spoken of and accepted in a non-judgmental way. No matter what the naturalist may say about the temperament or nature of the animal, I feel better when thinking of a dolphin.

As I said before when looking at Judgment, the Christian tradition does not easily fit this framework. I have placed Sacrament at this point to balance the Living Word of God. It certainly holds the concept of Mercy or Grace that is so difficult to rationally explain or preach upon. It is the hidden working of God at the deeper level of healing of the soul. It does not need a stated belief, but an acceptance, humility and sense of forgiveness, no matter what the person has done in the past. Repentance and remorse make way for an inner communion that defies explanation or logic. The Word or Gospel is spoken and demands a reaction - that is the masculine Evangelism. The Sacrament works at the unspoken feeling of Grace.

The correspondences in myth and legends are once again most difficult to portray. Persephone might best represent the modern Matrix personality, as well as in the Greek mythology, while in the Arthurian legend possibly Guinevere fits. Within the Robin Hood system, I am left with the most uncomfortable

Will Scarlet deputizing here. I can find no other!

5. Point of Reflection

Before I look at the next position on the Qabalah, I think it best to reflect for a few moments upon the whole framework so far.

As the picture has gradually built up it becomes apparent that the whole is in a continual tension. All the points are pulling against all the others. That is the nature of the subconscious mind, for remember it is a danger to consider the aspects in isolation. The mind is one. It is just a convenience to look more closely at the various areas of experience in the way we are doing.

The tension is more acute with regard to the distinct levels, for there lays its direct opposite in attribute. If the balance is out of true then it is usually seen as a vice, but if the balance is kept then it is a virtue. So if Aggression is dominant then that person may be regarded as a threat; if Feeling is dominant then they may be regarded as spineless; if the balance is true then the person is respected as sympathetic, but not a push-over. Similarly if Judgment is dominant then the person is usually regarded as cold hearted and lacking humanity; if Mercy is dominant then they are usually regarded as being somewhat useless or vaporous; if the balance is kept then the virtue is one of clarity of thought and heart.

One worrying reflection at this point is that I am sure most people are virtually unaware of what lies within them. The inner workings of the mind for them are a complete mystery or something best left to the professionals. That, to my mind, is an abrogation of responsibility. It is *our* lives so it is surely *our* responsibility to understand ourselves, our motivations, our weaknesses, our limitations and strengths. We need to come to terms with our fears, delight in our joys, work through our anxieties, widen our vision and dreams and grow towards fulfilling our potential. That means that, unfortunately for most people, even the first position of Aspiration remains a closed door! It takes courage to open the door in the exercise and discover what lies immediately behind it. Or again, a maze may be a fun thing to try for a Sunday afternoon at a theme park but, for most people, to consider it as a serious challenge of personal growth is an absurd notion!

My experience has shown me that most people do not want to look within. It is too frightening a prospect. The result is that most of my work with clients revolves around the therapeutic visualizations and not those of self awareness. Generally people are quite prepared to jog along and do no personal growth work at all, unless a problem presents itself. That is why the therapeutic exercises of the lower emotional level and interfaces are the most used of all. Finding the courage to face anxiety, or work towards rebirth from the subterranean puzzle of the subconscious, may be as far as some will venture. Buried anger and aggression of the Weather Queen can be easily understood, as is coping with pain and suffering in the Strength and Peace of the Tor. Self-confidence and strength might be sought to help heal repressed early experiences in Life, and can usually be achieved through the central Tree of the Perfect Balance Point, but to venture any higher in the Qabalah framework stays in the realms of "There be dragons"! That remains in the unknown fastness of the strange New Age weirdoes or Old Age fanatics and dreamers.

Let me get on my soapbox for a moment! Just by regarding people's actions you can have some idea as to the levels that people generally operate from, and gain a clue as to their lack of wholeness or personal growth.

I recognize that I am a cynic, but a cynic is not necessarily a pessimist. A cynic is much more likely to be a realist, even if saddened and slightly depressed by Life's experiences to date.

However, it seems to me that when talking with the general public the most self-acclaimed honor encountered is that of being fair minded and compassionate, and of not being swayed by emotionalism and jingoism. I am sure that we would all like to think we are of that ilk and, further more, are spiritually mature – some of us even "on their last reincarnated life" [if you believe in such things]! Even so, I am convinced that it is actually just emotion that is the main motivating factor in humanity's 'progress'. It seems to me that Self-interest dominates all things, despite any high sounding altruism. Altruistic justice, mercy and compassion are usually only given lip service, trotted out by politicians and the like to further their political ends, rather than coming from a genuine desire to provide for the helpless or needy. Justification of the deed, even if that deed remains solely in the realms of visualization, is most prominent [and earnestly believed!] – whilst honesty is very much a lone traveler. You see, cynicism abounds.

For some few brave souls the next Qabalah position is the zenith of their Aspirational Journey. Unfortunately, they fail to see this is not the ultimate goal of the Journey. However, to mistake the touching of the supernal level with the submerging within it, is understandable. This is especially so given the trouble in getting this far or coping with the darkness and pain encountered along the way. It is not a pleasant experience, for Life is full of Danger, Evil and Darkness as well as Light, Love and Joy. To try to attain the wonderful without meeting the abhorrent, is not only a false dream of the spiritually naïve but a dangerous and doomed venture of unseen pitfalls. The "Dark Night of the Soul" is a necessary experience of the Pilgrim, so let us proceed!

6. Visualizations continued

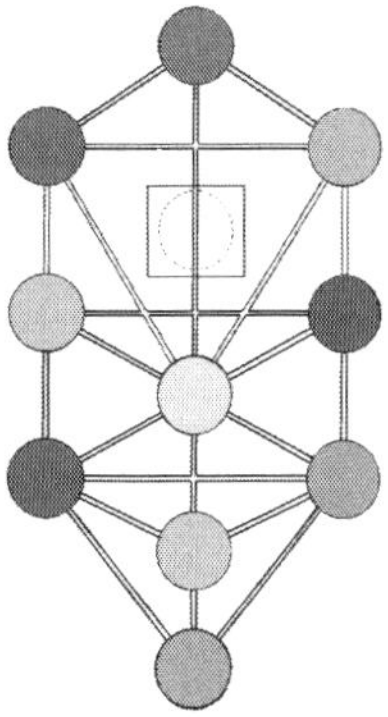

viii. The Hidden Point - The Abyss - Initiation

The last position that was explored along the neutral or dynamic equilibrium column was the Perfect Balance Point or Atonement. Although the therapeutic use was very clearly identifiable, notice there was no separate exercise for the magical use. The magical and self-awareness exercise was the same. In fact as we gradually move 'up' the Qabalah we note that this happens more frequently and exercises double-up. The Weather Queen and River of Life, when used together, could be usefully employed in a joint setting. Certainly both the Judgment and Mercy therapeutic and magical exercises did the same thing. Now, we find that for *the first time, all three uses* can combine, not only within a single setting, but within a single exercise as well.

You may recall that I had reservations at the construction stage of the Qabalah framework when considering this position. Logic demanded a position of interface between the Spiritual level and the Rational, but there was no easy answer as to why it had to be 'hidden'. Certainly convention calls upon such a classification and yet this position could well be the most significant position for any Seeker of advancement. For that reason I fail to truly understand why it cannot be called into the 'open'. Possibly the darkest or deepest secret that the Seeker may discover whilst on the Journey may be revealed here, so, to my way of thinking, it does not deserve the quality of Hiddenness that this position holds. However, significant and ground-breaking it most certainly is, and the titles of 'Abyss', 'Initiation' and 'Life or Death' are well justified.

Even more important now, as the Qabalah ascent is undertaken, is the absolute need for honesty in self-assessment. To self-delude at these latter stages is a waste of everyone's time and effort. To accept the exercise lesson is the best way to advance, no matter how unpalatable the information is. DO NOT DELUDE YOURSELF.

Often what little is known by the dilettante of this position is held in awe or a degree of anxiety. All of the positions can be uncomfortable or downright distressing if truly engaged upon, but this position usually holds a fascination and unhealthy dread! However, let me most hastily point out that all the positions involve change and growth within. That is the very raison d'etre of the Qabalah, and growth invariably involves pain or anxiety. As the saying goes, "no pain – no gain", but the 'pain' turns 'breakdown' of the counseling situation into 'breakthrough', and crucifixion to resurrection - death to life – and so on. However, *I must warn you that the next exercise would have an 'X' rating if it was shown as a film or on TV,* so if you have a nervous disposition or feel that violence is not for you, then you might find it too much to cope with. Yet violence is part of life, so I urge you to bite the bullet and proceed.

This is not a parlor game to enjoy if you are bored or fed up with the TV; this is not a hobby to indulge in or drop if other things take your fancy; this is not something "nice" that "nice people" do; this is foul, dirty, and degrading, for life can be foul, dirty and degrading. This is about life and cannot be avoided.

Up to this point there has always been the notion of being able to hold back until ready. Procrastination is a very useful ploy for the wary and can be played with a high degree of skill. It works for a while up to this point, even though the Journey once begun cannot really be stopped. Now the angels and demons must be faced, but whether they reside inside or have intrinsic 'outside' reality is really not the question. They must be challenged and not run from. They must be understood for what they can do, even if they are not understood for what they are. You are entering the realm of the supernal and great light and great darkness abides there. Once entered there is absolutely no escape. Enter at the peril of your soul.

Self-Awareness

The initial setting for this exercise has as its basis the West Kennet Barrow near Avebury. The pathway is a figment of imagination!

"Close your eyes and once again let the consciousness move from the possible physical points of intrusion, to the picture gradually developing in the inner world of the subconscious.

Before you even open your inner mental eyes, let me tell you what to expect. You will find a door – any kind of door – set in a stone wall. Perhaps it is even the same door, or design of door, you had for the very first exercise. So open your mental eyes and examine the door, and know that behind it is an underground cave or space in almost total darkness.

Open the door – step through – close the door behind you and take stock of what you see and experience. Although you can see so very little of what is around you, the overwhelming impact of that place is the smell. It is the smell of death and decay. Foul rotting bloated corpses must be in this place, for surely it is a place of death – a crypt or catacomb for the dead – and recently added to.

Try to breathe through the mouth to lessen the impact of its awfulness. Breathe shallowly and focus your attention on sight rather than smell.

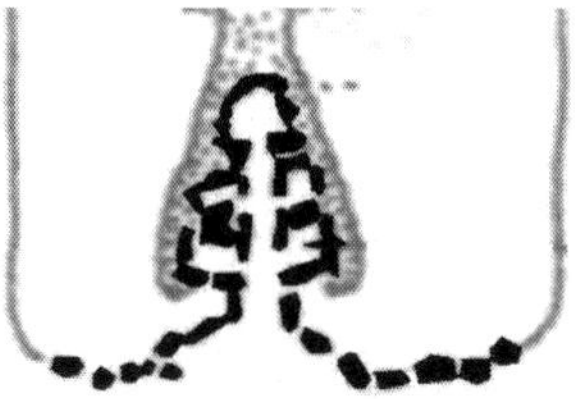

There are several smaller chambers lying off the main space in which you stand. Count them and discover there are five. You realize they form the stylized outline of the most ancient Earth Mother figure and you are standing at the throat position. You cannot help but take in the many corpses lying around and the piles of bones in each chamber. The place reeks and heaves with noisome movement and activity. Obviously you are not the only inhabitant in this place. There are foraging animals at hand.

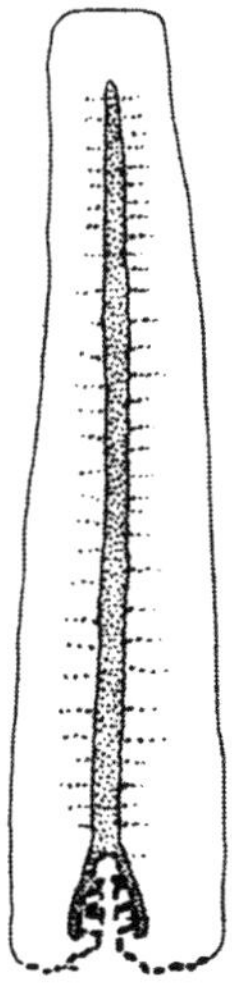

Look towards the entrance and sense, rather than see, a crone guarding the way in and out. Move towards her, and upon closer inspection you quail before the figure presented to you. She is hideous in aspect. Deformed and misshapen, filthy in the extreme, she is the epitome of the witch or hag. Without a word being said, you instinctively know that if you are to leave this place you must honestly, sincerely and ungrudgingly embrace her as a gesture of respect! If you truly cannot do this, turn around and locate the door back to your daily life. Do not even try to fool yourself. Be brutally honest. If you cannot do this, then take it as a sign that you are not ready to advance. If that is the case, then open the door and come back to your body and normal wakeful state, only trying to resume this exercise on a different day when you feel better about the whole experience.

If you can truly and un-hypocritically embrace the woman, then do so. She steps aside, so venture out of the barrow. Look at the strange world that greets you. From this moment on you are committed.

There is a strange quality to the air and color. It is difficult to put your finger on it, but it is almost as if this world is on a precipice of expectation and everything is accentuated as a result. The atmosphere is one of startling clarity and almost dances with hidden energy and electricity. There is an abnormal stillness as if Nature now holds her breath in anticipation. The whole world is looking to you and how you react or move.

The barrow is situated in a shallow valley with two paths leading away from it. The one on the right is on dry land, but the other to the left proceeds through a swamp of reed and sedge grasses. You perversely choose the left hand path and pick your way from clump to clump of quaking grass root islands that constitute the pathway here. The air is heavy, humid and hot. Sometimes you slip and mire your feet and legs and you can hear slithering sounds above the rustling of the reeds, so you know that animals or other creatures mark your progress although you cannot see them at all. Gradually, you make your way through the swamp to higher ground, emerging from that fetid place to stand upon a gravel path that follows a small rill, which feeds the swampland.

Wash your feet in the flowing water and rest for a while as you contemplate the way ahead.

A cowled figure, a monk or nun perhaps, walks slowly down the path to join you – beckons you follow - turns and retraces its steps. Do you trust this figure? Are you sure that the figure means you well? Do you accept this person as your Guide? Whether you join willingly, reluctantly or decide to wait a while to give space between you, you rise and make your way up the slope of the pathway. It slowly ascends to the valley ridge - and all the while the sense of expectancy increases.

The view from the ridge is rather bizarre. The path descends into what appears is a sea of darkness. It is as if the sunshine cannot penetrate below a certain level from the ridge top. If you are to proceed, you must accept the figure's reassurance that the pathway will not lead you to your doom. It is that or return the way you came, but even with that thought, as you look behind you, the path you walked so securely upon, now shimmers and changes shape. It looks more like that quagmire you thought you had left behind, so far below in the valley bottom. Even if you do not trust the cowled figure you now have to go forward, either on your own or together, in faith or trepidation, the way forward is really Hobson's choice.

Proceed down into the gloom and keep your wits about you. A growing quietness descends upon your progress. You can make noises by shouting, scuffing your shoes or clapping your hands together, but with the growing sense of dread with every step you take it seems a good idea to make as little noise as possible anyhow. Surely there is danger ahead. In the growing darkness what little vegetation there was quickly dies away. There is a deadness and dryness to the valley that seeps into the marrow of you bones. It is not coldness, just a great unease of 'deadness' and alienation to Life.

The valley bottom is reached and your 'guide' leads you into a deserted village from yesteryear. Even in the deep gloom or darkness you can still see the litter and decay of a medieval wattle and daub village, everything falling down and going to rack and ruin all around you. There has been no care or maintenance done to these hovels for a very long time. There are some animals here. They pick over the living and the dead of their fellow creatures. You sense a growing revulsion that is near to physical nausea, but you continue to follow your guide along the main path or roadway between the dwellings.

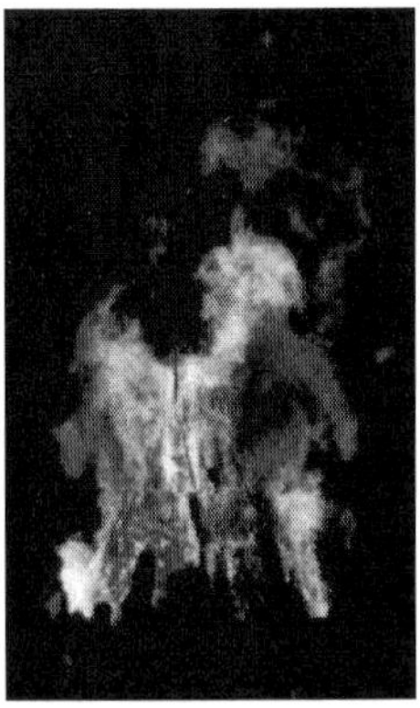

At the far end of the village, and a bit of a way off to one side, you see the light from a large bonfire. You both draw parallel to the light, but remain on the pathway and, unseen by those around the fire, you observe with growing horror the spectacle that unfolds before you. Here are the citizens of the village, if that is what you can call them. Bestial at times in appearance, they have gathered at this place and centered themselves around the fire leaving a fair space in the light for the central activity to take place. A naked youth has been tied to an upright pillar of wood, his hands bound behind him. Several naked maidens dance around him, weaving a complex dance in the open space, intently watched by the rest of the people. Their bodies look so white, yet their hair is universally black

and long. There is a perverseness about them that is difficult to define, but they hold a fascination that demands attention. Almost on the verge of perception you sense, rather than see, spectral figures or ghouls looking on from further out from the activity of the village inhabitants. The feeling of dread increases.

One of the maidens picks up a golden sickle and bowl and advances to the youth. With careless expertise she castrates the youth with a single sweep, catching the blood and offering in the bowl.

With revulsion and desperate horror uppermost, turn away from the soul-sickening sight and gladly follow the beckoning guide away and upwards from the evil scene of the last few moments. As you gradually ascend out of that dreadful valley the darkness lightens, vegetation begins to appear and normal sounds of life can be heard around you.

You attain the valley ridge and look back into that strange looking 'sea of darkness', letting the horror of the last few minutes fall away. Compare that past valley with the next that has opened up before you. The vista that lies ahead is one of extreme sharp contrast. This valley looks to be filled with a glowing light. Everything is enhanced in some way. Everything seems crystal clear, bright and full of exquisite detail!

With such a heightened air of delight, you most gladly follow your guide now down the pathway into the next valley, your heart forgetting the recent horror and warming with each new sight that greets your eyes. As you descend, the very air becomes alive with life. You feel warm and relaxed, content and wonderfully safe. There is the sound of life all around and water is dancing nearby. There is an abundance of variety of every species within creation. Everything bursts with life - the trees, shrubs, flowers, insects, birds and tiny creatures and animals. It is beautiful.

As you near a clearing of silky grass sward to one side of the pathway, a circle of stones comes into view. In the center, sitting cross-legged and twirling strands of grass around her fingers, is a beautiful naked maiden. She has long blond hair curled around her shoulders and she seems to be waiting for something or someone.

There is movement further away beyond the circle which the maiden espies. She stands and looks that way expectantly, her tresses flowing down her back. She sees a naked Adonis coming her way and she waves a greeting to him. He runs the last few yards to the edge of the circle and, both of them oblivious to your presence; she invites him to join her at the center of the grassy area. They embrace and begin to make love. There is such an aura of tenderness and desire that, with the greatest respect, you turn away to look elsewhere. Your guide has anticipated your reaction and bids you continue along the pathway.

As the path begins to ascend out of this most wonderful valley you experience a wave of love of life, to which everything around you responds. You presume that the couple in the circle have climaxed in their love-making and this is somehow shared and felt by every living thing in the vicinity. There is now a sense of deepening appreciation of life that is beyond your ability to voice or conceptualize. It is just felt at the deepest level of your heart.

The path reaches the ridge of this valley of life and you look beyond to the descent, to see once again the barrow and swamp. You have journeyed full circle, for this is the other pathway you saw at the beginning. As you turn to make some comment to your guide you realize that that person has disappeared! You are quite alone. With a casual air you slowly descend, knowing that your soul has just received an extremely important lesson. It is one that will have a profound effect upon you, but also one that will take many an hour's deliberation to begin to truly appreciate.

You approach the barrow expecting to see the hag guarding the way back to your normal life, but as she stands and looks towards you, her form changes and flows. The hag becomes a heavily pregnant mature woman, and then changes again to become the beautiful maiden of the circle of stones. She smiles and welcomes you – you embrace – and she allows you entrance to the barrow.

Expecting the noisome spectacle that you experienced before, you surprisingly find the barrow smelling of fresh air and a hint of wild flowers. It is clear of corpses and bones. It is dry underfoot and quite empty.

Finding the door that will return you to your normal world, you take one final look around you, open the door, step through, close the door and let that image gently shimmer and fade away.

In your own time open your eyes".

In my opinion it is foolishness to consider that spiritual attainment can be achieved only by thinking of the Light, praising God and mouthing platitudes on every occasion. Life is never a thing of clean hands but dirt, hard work and a mix of joy and sorrow, heights and depths, living and dying. To expect only sweetness and light, or to see that as an expression of spiritual growth, is a sure sign of living in a Fool's Paradise. If that is the way you believe things to be, then you must grow up and see the world as it truly is.

We can no longer operate from the point of indecision. Commitment is being called for to enter fully upon the spiritual path. Once a decision is made there can be no turning back, no second choice. Although the sense of this was given as long ago as the Maze exercise, there was always the chance of 'slowing down', of being so caught up with survival in this world that spiritual growth could be put on hold for a while. If you completed this exercise there is no time to relax or take a holiday. The spiritual journey continues without reprieve. You cannot opt out for *any* reason. You realize at some inner level that everything that happens to you has its spiritual lesson to impart, and how you react to it has consequences that defy the logical mind. There can only be a proceeding to greater light or greater darkness. There is no middle ground. That is the understanding of Initiation. That is the inner meaning of the Adam and Eve story. Once the fruit of knowledge has been eaten it cannot be 'un-eaten'. It might be unpalatable, or even regurgitated, but it cannot be 'un-eaten'. There is only the consequences left of every action undertaken, seen from the 'godlike' perception of spiritual awareness – of knowledge of right and wrong. That is the onus of true spiritual advancement.

As this position is worked upon, the spiritual distinctions become more urgent. They might not become clearer or more polarized, but they certainly become more clamorous. Integrity is sparked off here. A sureness of direction grows, yet a defined code of ethics will not. Such does not magically appear, for such a code belongs to the conscious mind and we are developing spirituality that belongs in the subconscious. However, an inner sense of rightness or righteousness, of spirituality and spiritual awareness is being sought. The Abyss is passed and there is no going back.

Who did you relate to or find the greatest affinity with? Was it the sacrificed youth, the crowd, the dancing maidens, the lovers, or none or all of them? Did you have any fascination with the macabre? Did you want to be a voyeur? Where you caught by stereotypes and prejudices? Inspect your inner secrets and embrace them! Perhaps they might not be such dreadful ghoulish apparitions as you first imagined. Perhaps by inspection and acceptance they not only become full of promise of new life and of change, but transform into understanding of something quite different. That is the miracle of this position. It is not something to be afraid of, but respect and embrace as the deeper meaning of Life - and progress.

Therapeutic Involvement and Magical Use

As I said before, there are no separate visualizations for the therapeutic or magical use. It is all a-oneness of a tremendous importance to accept yourself, your potential, your gifts, limitations and weaknesses. In the acceptance and understanding there is the beginning of wisdom and new birth. There is no alternative to growth.

Legend, Myth and Religious Comparisons

There is no 'Yetziratic Text' to peruse for this point. This Sephirah of Daath is a comparative newcomer and not part of a long mystical tradition. It may be implied by logical deduction, but it has no reality within the Jewish Mystical tradition. The Jewish Qabalah is a framework for understanding the nature of God. "God is Light and in Him is no darkness at all". With that understanding there can be no position of such polarity. From the perspective of human kind, God may at times appear to be a God of Wrath and Capricious in nature - even 'dark' that needs placating, but for the Jew that concept is beyond the pale. There can be no darkness in God. His people might need repentance and atonement for their sins, but that is not the fault of God but the people. The Testament is clear. Justice will prevail as understanding grows, but evil has no part in the nature of the godhead. Hence there is no place for such a Sephirah. It is a later Qabalistic necessary invention to understand the nature of creation, and mankind in particular, but not the nature of the Creator. Although it is itself many hundreds of years old it is not as old as the original Qabalah, and so is another reason I am not afraid to go against the convention of that day!

I have placed Uranus at this point. Astrologically, the planet is quite modern as it was not discovered until a couple of centuries ago! It certainly holds the Karmic, and possibly violent, connotations of this position. There is a perversity to Uranus and a sense of the individual that encapsulates the individual's self imposed suffering to gain revelation and spiritual advancement. It is the lonely journey of the dark night of the soul, represented by this planet, which has been foretold from times past, for each person born to this world and this fated nature of spiritual growth has also to be embraced in some way.

The Tarot is a symbolic framework of understanding of experience. Death is the most obvious card, for it opens the way for rebirth and new life of understanding. You cannot better this simple statement for this position.

I have placed the snake as the animal here. It is hardly a new idea, for that animal holds such mystical attraction, with potentially fatal consequences, that it has been used for such symbolism from time immemorial. The original Adam and Eve story uses the snake in this way and I cannot find a better creature symbol.

In the Arthurian legend, I believe that the actual quest of the Holy Grail best represents this position. Therefore, the cup itself, as well as the never ending quest, can correspond. The quest is not as clearly defined a correspondence as symbols in the other positions, as it is quite a vague concept in this context, but the cup is a symbol itself of the quest and might be carefully used within the fable.

The Sheriff of Nottingham, or even the castle itself, might correspond within the Robin Hood legends whilst Mr Smith deputizes within the Matrix set.

Aspects of Loki, the Norse mythology, fit the bill, as do aspects of Skiva in the Hindu. Any of the darker figures have the power to represent here, such as Set or Satan or Lucifer. Even the generalizations of ghouls, vampires and soul destroying spirits might correspond. It is how they are placed in their respective contexts that give them the power to work and not be just childish figures to frighten the credulous.

The Christian tradition is probably the most used tradition of all in the West to speak of such moments - and not necessarily used only by the religious. The cross and crucifixion are such potent symbols, that anyone in any kind of deep suffering identifies with the Christ on the Cross. They might not embrace

Christianity, but it cannot be ignored. The extreme suffering unto death has been looked up to over the centuries as an example of such selflessness and sacrifice, that even the most ardent anti-church protagonist might use it to express their inner turmoil and pain on occasions.

As a Christian ordained priest I am greatly tempted to use this as an evangelical platform and speak of the difference between the Gnostic position and that of the Christian. I bite my tongue and do not fall into the trap, for I would be going against the principles I presented at the beginning of this work. This writing is not an evangelical opportunity, but an exposition of the Qabalah and an attempt to rid the framework of specific religiosity! No doubt I will be held to account over this in the future.

ix. The God Within - Wisdom and Karma

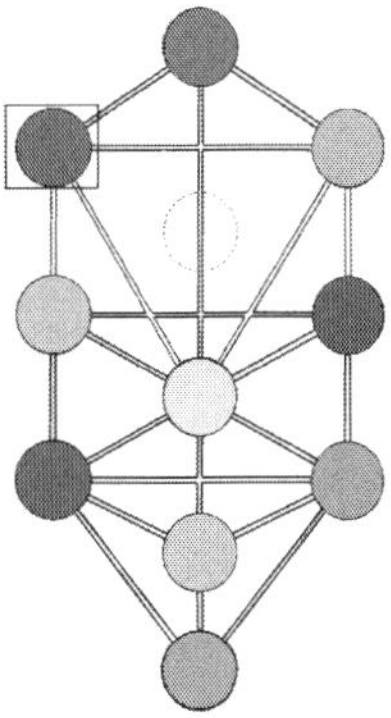

The Abyss was the position where good and evil were encountered. Note I did not say right and wrong, for good might appear right but in fact later be understood as wrong, and evil might at first appear wrong but later be seen to be right. That is where interpretation and the conscious mind is involved. We are only trying to explore the subconscious and direct experience or encounters with the concepts of spirituality – hence good and evil and not right and wrong.

Having passed the Abyss with all its connotations of darkness and responsibility, it comes as a most pleasant surprise to find that the supernal levels are all they promise to be.

The next two positions epitomise 'Force' and 'Form', but do keep in mind that the masculine attribute associated with this colomn is not the testosterone charged aggression of the Weather Queen, nor the single-minded determination of Judgment, but the high sense of integrity and motivation that has connotations of conscience, morals, ethics and duty. It is a state of readiness that implies an impending action that, once started, is not going to stop until wrongs are righted, justice prevails and the spiritual quest is resumed and restored. I offer two thoughts for the top of the masculine 'Force' column to help understand further.

Firstly, a most cynical but not original statement is that "The one thing that history teaches us is that we never learn anything from history!" Unfortunately, the truth of that statement is clear for all to see with regards to 'en masse'. Again and again we see the same trends and fashions coming round and round once more. It seems that human nature never changes, even though society, its technologies and politics, inevitably alters all the time. Kingdoms rise and fall, empires come into prominence and then gradually fade from view. It is a certainty that "there isn't anything new under the Sun" as far as human nature is concerned.

Thank the Lord that that is not true for an individual. Despite my cynicism, I still have the most positive outlook for individuals and believe that each person has an almost infinite capacity for growth and change – and a learning process is mainly based on personal experience. A person may have to face the same challenge several times over before a lesson is truly learnt, but if that person wants to grow, then grow they will. Lessons may be hard and increase in severity until the lesson is learnt, but experience – or that individual's history – is the key to growth. More of that later.

To understand the second thought one needs to take into account the changing use of words over the centuries. In years gone by, especially in biblical times, a 'wise' carpenter was not necessarily someone who knew how to manage his work force well - good management of today - but one who understood his wood, its grain, strength and flexibility. He might have been an absolute tyrant as an employer, but, with a particular use held in mind, the wood would have been shaped to obtain the best for that piece. That was wisdom. It was something that came with experience, of years of working with all manner of woods and needs. It was not just a matter of knowledge, but knowledge and experience of many years standing. The result was a 'wise carpenter'.

What was true of carpenters was true of any tradesman or member of a profession. You would find wise stonemasons, wise scribes, wise cooks etc. Of course *in that sense,* a 'wise' *person* was someone who understood humankind - a sage. He or she would know how to produce harmony amidst conflict and order out of chaos.

Naturally this meant that wisdom could not possibly be the common experience of the young, but almost exclusively understood to be the perogative of the elderly. Years brought wisdom.

Further more, in those days wisdom could not be held without reference to God or the Divine. It was axiomatic that wisdom took into account human's dealings with Divinity. In fact, for most of recorded history, to be civilised meant that there was an established religion present. It also had to be a practical religion - whatever religion that one was - one that worked, and it would not have been possible to bring a stable society into existence without such a reference. A healthy society always needs a base upon which integrity and respect can be founded and for a sense of stability to be assured. Past civilisation could not result without this. That was the yardstick of a working religion. "To know God is the beginning of Wisdom".

However, you could not blame God if the wood snapped. You could not blame God if the building collapsed. You could not blame God if you had not prayed about a situation. Therefore, Wisdom was, and is, more than good Judgment - it is a gestalt of the whole of experience, with integrity and self respect most centrally placed and held with respect to 'something greater'. It is the 'octave' of the *human* Will from the Rational level and Judgment position to the spiritual level or 'Will of God' position - religiously speaking [of course!] - sometimes referred to as Karma.

Non-religiously speaking, if the medium upon which work is to be done for the carpenter is wood, then the medium upon which you are to work is yourself, your own subconscious. It is the whole of your self that now must be examined, understood and enabled. It involves every aspect of you - with integrity at its heart.

However, once a mistake is recognized then Integrity requires a response. To know that something needs to be put right demands an action. To get this far on the Journey of Life demands the response to grow. Knowledge and good judgment are insufficient. Growth is a MUST – 'Force' needs to be liberated.

Possibly the most profound and debatable point I make is that I do not see Integrity as an attribute that is earned. Moral and ethical codes are things of the conscious mind, and can be developed and worked upon consciously. Through conscious understanding, conscience can be 'pricked', but that still remains a conscious process. We are looking below the conscious, within the subconscious mind. This is the home of guilt and remorse, and integrity is allied and very present. Guilt may be felt because of moral codes instilled and programmed through conscious effort, but it is integrity that promises doing something about it. Integrity may be moribund. It may need coercion and cajoling through guilt, but I believe it is present in every human being anyhow. In that sense, it is god given by virtue of being alive. It may just need to be acknowledged and freed to act.

One could say that the measure of spirituality is the strength or depth of integrity.

It is the purpose of this exercise not just to awaken the appreciation of wisdom, but to foster the same by an objective view of personal history. You might not agree with the doctrinal or philosophical position, but that is almost incidental. The symbols are what are important here rather than the belief concept being presented. Even if the doctrine of Reincarnation is not embraced, there is no reason why the looking back at this life cannot be the same spur.

Self-Awareness

The idea for this exercise has its origins in a painting by psychic medium artist Joyce Betts-Lambert. I would love to own it!

"Close your eyes and once again let the consciousness move from the possible physical points of intrusion, to the picture gradually developing in the inner world of the subconscious.

Find yourself standing upon a windswept escarpment, where the folded rock outcrops in a wide upsweep of layers, jutting out over an immense valley floor with its breath-catching panorama. There is a distinct feeling of everything alien present, for the sky is red, as is most of the land open upon view. There are clouds in the sky and trees and vegetation, but everything looks strange. The normal terrestrial colors are not present or not quite what you would expect. There is no overall green and blue as on Earth. The dominant colors are red and brown, as if the land is in pain or on fire, struggling to survive in a most hostile environment. However, it seems that all hangs together as a whole, even though the colors are not those expected in normal life. It all fits together in that alien sense of rightness. It is almost as if the planet Mars has migrated to Earth, bringing all its red soil, sky and sharply pointed land features. Yet there is no trouble breathing the air in this place, and gravity seems the same as Earth. No problem or physical discomfort exists. You stand in meditative pose looking out over the vast plain and vista.

In general, the view that greets your eyes is one of desert and perpetual dryness – an aridity that no doubt denies the chance of life to gain a foothold. There are many outcrops of rock with different shades of red indicating different areas of soil or land mass, but nothing is seen that indicates life of any kind. There is no change of terrain, just smaller boulders, rocks and color change that show, although in an infinite variety of guises, the forever-same deadness or absence of life. Yet wending its way across the alien desert is a clearly observed path and roadway. At least along a thin strip of pathway are signs of life and green vegetation.

You realize that the sense of the alien is even associated with the path, for it takes a most unnatural route across the valley. It consists of strips of pathway that are essentially straight, although of differing lengths of straightness, and the whole forms a zigzag through the desert in a bizarre and unnecessarily long fashion. The whole journey to your present position is many, many times longer than is necessary to simply traverse the desert.

Looking more closely at an individual straight section, you can see

fairly clearly a well-defined road. There may be obstacles that the road has to dodge around, or signposts and junctions that quickly lead into the nothingness of the desert, but there is no mistaking the road taken to this point. It is the only path of life. Upon closer inspection, you can begin to discern patterns to the obstructions and junctions, as if the road is duplicating the experience of passage in some way. Differences of size of obstruction or overall length of obstruction are discernable, yet the sense of sameness is kept that must be contrived or thought out by its creator. There are patterns here that need exploring.

Upon this vantage point of the escarpment, as you look back upon the route you must have taken, you instinctively understand that you expected to see the repeating patterns. You expected to see duplication and unnecessary mileage. You expected to see a zigzag of untold miles. You expected to see false paths and useless signs. You expected to see only one successful route to this place. It is your route to the Here and Now! Just how many zigzags have you made? How many lifetimes have been spent learning and relearning lessons? How many more lifetimes lie before you?

Rest your eyes upon the whole, taking in as much of the scene in a single sweep of appreciation. Your past is reviewed before you, laid down as a route followed through the dryness of death. It is the Journey of Life in symbolic form. It is the route YOU have taken. It is your unique path of progress, with all its hurdles and lessons learnt or re-learnt. In humility, accept the waste of effort. With an air of contriteness and remorse turn to face the way forwards. With an inner conviction to try again with renewed effort, be prepared to continue your Journey. Learn from what you have seen before you. It is time to travel on.

Let that image gently shimmer and fade away. Return to the here and now and in your own time open your eyes."

The symbolism is self-evident. Within that understanding of reincarnation, each turn represents a new life or incarnation with its lessons and karma to be worked upon. If lessons are not learnt the first time, then they need to be repeated or emphasized until they are taken on board. If justice is not played out during one lifetime, then the need or opportunity to repay is found in another. The symbolism suggests that progress may be sporadic or very hardly won, but progress is the end result.

Yet this is much more than just a 'time out' opportunity. The understanding of challenge, progress and past mistakes made through one's own lack of integrity or effort, leads to a deep yearning to put things right. There cannot be a time of rest until such an attempt has been made. It is the spur to try again and again and again – to grow. The up welling of energy and motivation is the fundamental response or consequence to such knowledge. Personal integrity demands no less. "There is no rest for the wicked"!

It is when a person has the privileged opportunity to be able to review past progress that a sense of purpose, humility and understanding dawns at the subconscious appreciation level. It is not a matter of doctrinal belief or evaluation of different faiths, but a soul-level 'knowing' of infinite time and growth of the soul. Truly we all are 'sons of the most High' – or in other words – 'Children of God', or even in one sense - gods incarnate here on Earth. That sense of great purpose is what is being evoked through this exercise.

Therapeutic Involvement

There can be no healing of the spirit in the sense of healing the body or mind when required. The divine spark within - the Light that lighteth every man - is the 'Perfect' indestructible part of the person that continues throughout time and eternity. It may need to be freed from the shackles of suffering, sinfulness and earthbound selfishness, but it has no need to be healed. In this position, when we consider the masculine 'god' within, awareness and understanding of our place in the great scheme of things is the gateway to spiritual growth and freedom, especially when we consider our relationship to the Divine. I am not evaluating the various doctrines of atonement. That is a thing of the conscious mind. I am inviting the deeper self to examine that relationship and wondrous journey to the Light. With that understanding, there is no real difference between self-awareness and therapeutic development.

The Therapeutic and Self Awareness uses must be considered as one and the same. Just by repeated use of this visualization, memories of past lives or past times may come unbidden. Dreams of these times might become more frequent. A sense of 'at home' might steal upon you when you think of a specific time or place. However, it can be tuned more acutely and the escarpment be used as a starting place to 'hone in' on particular zigzags, obstacles or false routes. Using a 'telescope' of the mind's eye, they can be examined for symbolic or even straight picture content, and with understanding comes acceptance, forgiveness and the desire to atone or make good. It is a way of looking at the Akashic Records of your soul's progress through this or several lifetimes, if you accept that doctrine. It is a way of healing memories in this lifetime anyhow, or in past lives, if that is acceptable in your belief system.

Magical Use

It is possible to use the principles of that exercise in a far more general manner. What is done specifically for you as an individual, can be accomplished for anyone or anything. It also does not have to be looking back at a Lifeline as in the above exercise, but in a manner that best suits your skills and 'bent'. Some of you will prefer the pictorial 'snapshot' review of a family photo album. Some will prefer a more formal venture into a 'virtual library'. Whatever system you might use, it may be symbols are seen. It may be photographs or moving pictures that are seen. It may be text that appears and needs to be read or interpreted. Any manner of the above may present itself, or a mixture of them or refinement.

Have a go at this, but I suggest that instead of looking back and viewing progress as a series of symbols, a more formal and distinctive approach be tried. Try to find out what caused the particular tragedy to the submarine "Thresher" as an attempt to get this point across.

"Close your eyes, let the normal background noises and distractions

fade away, and turn your attention to your inner world.

Find yourself in the foyer of a large Library. There is no one around. The place is empty but warm and well lit. You are here to find out what really happened to the submarine "Thresher" when it went missing in the early 60's.

Every library is laid out most logically with divisions and subdivisions by author or subject. Walk around the Reception area and enter the Reference section of the building. According to your way of thinking, refine your search amongst the shelves by either looking for the history, naval history, naval mysteries or marine disasters section. You may like to use the cataloguing system or just browse the shelves, but look for the subject of "Thresher" or its equivalent.

Refine your search even further by finding your data in the form that you prefer. Choose as to whether you see this as a book, data CD/DVD, floppy disc or its equivalent, either sitting down to read the book or file, view it as a micro-fiche, or to be played on a PC placed for that very purpose. Access the data and find out what happened.

Replace the data in its relevant niche. Clear up, so no one can see you have been present. Return to the Reception area, let the image gradually shimmer and fade away as you return to the here and now.

In your own time open your eyes."

Everything that has happened on this planet has left its record of event in the ether. This is the 'Akashic Record' that can be accessed by those with the gift. It is not dependent upon a particular method to enable access of information. It is important to find the method that suits you - provided you have the psychic gift in the first place. However, it is by exercising this position of the Qabalah that such a gift may be discovered and trained. Take care, for information is power, and who is to say whether the information you receive this way is true, or whether it is just a figment of your wishful imagination!!

Insight in this situation comes from understanding the past.

It is Wisdom to learn. It is 'god-like' to have this ability. Adam and Eve were tempted to become 'godlike' and eat of the fruit of the tree of Knowledge. It is Christ-like to find tolerance, remorse, forgiveness and a need to endeavor to put wrongs right if you can! Integrity, along with the other positional abilities of Judgment, Compassion, Acceptance or Drive, need to combine in ways that bring 'wholeness' to the person. Jung's Individuation is engaged upon with a vengeance!

Legend, Myth and Religious Comparisons

The Jewish Qabalah was to try to understand the nature of God - not God's creation. This Sephirah of Chokmah, which I have left at its more accepted conventional position of the top of the Masculine Pillar [even though I have switched the Pillars around], translates as 'Wisdom', however, this is the wisdom of God and, as such, needs a deep understanding. It is not simply an extension of the biblical understanding as in the 'wise carpenter', applied to a supernal being. Here is the out-flowing, boundless energy of God, but used with infinite wisdom and understanding. God is the All-Knowledgeable - and God's Will will be done! There can be no outguessing of God. There can be no sidestepping the Will of God. Even within all the doctrinal arguments of Free Will and Predestination, of Karma and Love and Justice, yet there is still the underlying acceptance that somehow, throughout all history, God's Will is done. We may believe we have Free Will, but the paradox is that it is taken into account within God's scheme of things - and, of course, a paradox is beyond explanation. To seek knowledge of God at this level means to endeavor to understand the Will of God.

I have placed Saturn at this point. Astrologically, the planet has overlapping connotations with Uranus, but whereas Uranus may be regarded as the Lord of Karma, Saturn is the God of the World and Time. The awesome challenges that lead to soul's growth are governed by this planet – and do not simply apply to the individual. It is sometimes considered as the Great Malevolent, but only in the sense of what is needful for the ultimate good of the individual's, nation's or world's growth. An individual lifetime may seem to have been wasted or squandered, a nation may seem to be in decline, but somehow lessons of Karma have been incorporated, met or avoided.

The Tarot card I have chosen is the Hierophant or Pope. It enshrines the earthly representation of Wisdom and Holiness in human terms, even though, in reality, the human figure will never come up to the expectations of being Godlike. However, it is the use of symbolic correspondence that is being offered here – not the alternative to the Divine!

I have placed the Owl as the animal here. Once more, it is hardly a new idea. The Owl has epitomized wisdom within the animal kingdom for many an age. The correspondences are deep rooted in the human psyche, even if mainly within the Western experience. However, remember that this series of exercises and book was written for the Westerner and the Celt in particular.

In the Arthurian legend Merlin fits the bill. Although he is a magician, and could be placed at the Emotional level, he is best thought of as the person of Wisdom, who also happens to have magical ability.

King Richard might correspond within the Robin Hood legends, although that is beginning to push things to the limit, but The Architect does much to meet the special qualities within the Matrix set.

The other correspondences associated with past religions could be Pallas-Athene, a virgin goddess of wisdom issuing from Zeus or Isis-Urania within the Egyptian framework. Notice that these are female representatives, for once again we have the difficulty of gender and attribute mix.

Within the Christian tradition, I see the masculine column

triumphed as the Way of Faith or Salvation. Once again, I do not want to fall into the trap of discussion as to spiritual growth either by way of works or faith in Christ, but simply offer the correspondence of Salvation, as it is a response to God's love that leads to growth and deeper understanding of God's Will for each and every one of us. Unfortunately, *the* symbol of salvation cannot be used without recourse to doctrine somewhere along the line, even though the Cross is a talisman that crosses ethnic boundaries. It implies a living faith as well as a world wide religion, and that faith is a personal and conscious surrender of self to the Will of God and acceptance of Christ's sacrifice for Atonement.

x. The Goddess Within – Holiness, Serenity and Intuition

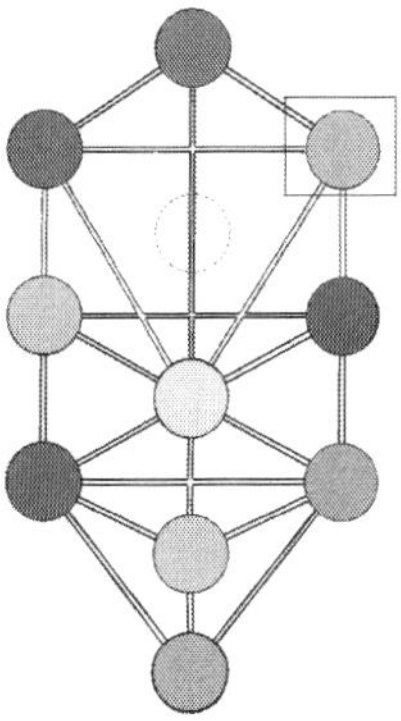

Like the other levels of Emotion and Rational thought, this level has the obvious tension between the masculine and feminine columns. The God within needs to be balanced by the Goddess within. 'Force' must be balanced by 'Form', and vice versa. So, whereas the God had connotations of action to maintain integrity or implement the Will of God or the God within, so the Goddess has connotations of being or resting in holiness. Furthermore, where integrity involves a moral and ethical *stance* that has grown from experiences of life, so holiness needs to forever have an eye on the future, for the *state* of holiness or Bliss could be dashed by wrongful actions. Wisdom results from a certain degree of knowledge, however, holiness or True Righteousness need not be knowledgable yet intuitively know what is right!

I normally quite deliberately do not use words such as Salvation or Grace or the jingles that accompany those Christian doctrines, however, I cannot avoid words that are often used in theology as I endeavour to clarify spirituality. The temptation is to speak about 'Original Righteousness' as well as the more usually known doctrine of 'Original Sin', but that would be going against the very principles that I am trying to follow. I aim to talk about spirituality *not* exclusively within the Christian context. Unfortunately Original Righteousness is also the area of understanding that I am trying to put into more commonly understood words.

Let me try to put it another way. At the previous position of Wisdom, although moral and ethical codes are placed within the conscious mind, the moral *stance* is what is appreciated and grows from Life's experiences. Integrity is there to be embraced and set free, for stance is the prelude to action. It is not earned but found within, and the measure of spirituality was the strength or depth of integrity.

Similarly with this position, the *state* of Holiness is not earned. It cannot be won through conscious effort, but it is something that is found or revealed to be present within. It is also god given by virtue of the person being alive. It also needs just to be embraced and delighted in. Therefore in this position, I see spirituality as something that develops and grows, like 'fruit of the spirit' – that is the *degree* of holiness. The *state* of holiness is something revealed, surrended to and accepted.

Another thing to keep in mind is that, whereas the masculine column always has the Sun as a correspondence, so the feminine column always has the Moon as its counterpart. Be careful, for there is much speculation as to how far such an analogy can be drawn. The Sun is the light giver, and although the Moon shines upon the Earth, it is only reflected light from the Sun. That being so, I believe that it is surely dangerous to take this analogy too far into the Qabalah symbolism. At its extreme it would minimise the feminine influence to the point that it is completely dependent upon the masculine, and I cannot sustain such a position in the face of feminine activism, let alone my own integrity! My wife would not allow it! Nevertheless, I will use this Moon correspondence and so offer the following exercise.

Self-Awareness

The idea for this exercise has its origins in my past regular practice of walking along the seashore, both day and night.

"Close your eyes and once again let the consciousness move from the

possible physical points of intrusion, to the picture gradually developing in the inner world of the subconscious.

Find yourself upon a very wide flat beach. The tide is out and you stand far from the dry land near the shoreline. It is a very, very still night. The stars are quite brilliant and fill the dark sky.

The waves are tiny. They plash so gently on the dim sand by your feet, hardly making a sound. Occasionally the water reminds you of its presence as it reaches and tickles your toes. Even so it is no intrusion, just a pulling you back to this inner world rather than allowing you to wander off in your mind.

You can see for miles along the beach as it stretches around an enormous bay. In the far distance a seaside town calls to you with its buzz of noise and twinkling lights.

The Moon is full and shines above the horizon, far out to sea. It leaves a silvery path across the water for you to follow.

There is no wind, not even a hint or whisper of movement. It is absolutely still all around you.

Here is peace, perfect peace.

Hold that image for as long as you feel comfortable. Drink it in. Live in the moment, the Peace, for peace is the sound of heaven on earth.

When it feels right to break the spell, look once more to the Moon. It hangs immense and full, and seems to draw you into itself. In fact, it could be that it is growing or you rise up towards it. Let go, release any anxiety and fall into its attraction.

As you float above the waters, let that image gently shimmer and fade away. Return to the here and now and in your own time open your eyes."

The symbolism is not complex. The sea represents your inner mind with all its currents and tides, its hidden depths and desires. It also has its connotations of the feminine. The seaside town is your daily life with its distractions and immediate clamor, calling even through your time of quiet and introspection. The peace that surrounds you is the Peace that "passes understanding", an inner resource freely given, never won, but forever fragile and vulnerable. The Moon represents your feminine Goddess, the Mother of your Soul, the Intuitive inner self.

To surrender is to evoke the Goddess, but once embraced she will never drop you, although She will never let you forget that the sanctity of your soul is your own responsibility. The Peace within is that which comes from Being in the Divine. It is Serenity or Holiness – it rests in your soul. Its fragility is your vulnerability, and a part of your understanding can never rest from such responsibility.

Therapeutic Involvement

As stated before, there can be no healing of the spirit in the sense of healing the body or mind if required. The spirit may need to be freed, but it never needs to be healed.

One danger to spiritual advancement is that of *Self*-Righteousness. The ego cannot stand to be wrong and it also needs constant strokes. To aid it in its delusions it becomes adept at hiding from accountability and responsibility. Self-righteousness is one of its most powerful tools at its disposal.

Once again, the Therapeutic and Self Awareness uses must be considered as one and the same. By repeated use of this exercise, the light of the Divine illuminates the inner light of the soul, be it its paucity or its richness. It is not a knowing of what needs to be done - that is Wisdom, but it is a knowing that either Peace is there – or it isn't! Self-Righteousness is shown up for what it truly is, and true humility grows in its place.

Magical Use

The magical use of the 'God' within is the exploration of the 'Akashic Record'. That is the record of *everything* that has happened in the *past.* Whether it fades with depth in time or becomes less and less accessible, I do not know, for less and less detail seems to be recoverable the further back the search is in time. I do know that if the practitioner is gifted, then it is a horrendously powerful tool that demands an integrity most of us cannot muster. Perhaps there lie its safeguards, checks and balances for it is beyond most people's reach to practice.

The magical use of the 'Goddess' within, is the divination of the *future.* Needless to say, it matches the power of the masculine column and demands no less of the moral and ethical stance that its counterpart enjoys. Although precognition can be a veritable lifesaver, the same checks and balances prevent exploitation for self-aggrandizement.

The setting and operation are very close to those employed within the magical setting of the 'River of Life' at the Emotional level. However, whereas the usage at that level is to divine the present, with its limitations and possible changes that can be made, the usage of the 'Goddess' is about that which is to come. It is the same paradox of the Will of God at the top of the masculine column, although to a much lesser degree. Somehow the future is divined, even though it is not fixed, if we believe we have free will. In fact, it was the mark of the true Prophet that the foretelling always came about. Nevertheless, prophecy and divination are notoriously fickle and have a habit of turning from true. It is a very brave or foolish person who puts unlimited store by such things. I suggest the following as a formal setting to exercise the gift.

"Close your eyes; let the normal background noises and distractions fade away, and turn your attention to your inner world.

You find yourself walking in almost total darkness along a woodland track that wends its way between the silent sentinels of Oak, Ash and towering Beech. Their sheer size and imposing grandeur invokes a sense of unease. It is as if they frown upon your intent and purpose, or at least question your reason for continuing. Be sure of yourself. Inspect your motivation, for you are here to consult the Oracle in this place.

You emerge upon the edge of a woodland clearing, just past the shadows and darkness of the trees, and stand in the light of the full moon. Ahead lay a circle of smallish stones wherein a woman stands tall and slender, dominating the enclosure with the strength of her presence. Her eyes see past your outer shape to the heart and secrets of your hidden self. It is obvious her world is different to yours. The sights she looks upon must be totally alien to your own. She is a goddess, a prophetess, a seer.

At her side is a bowl of crystal light, the magic of which she controls and loves. She bids you enter the circle and approach.

With hesitant steps you accept her invitation, although the prospect is daunting and humbling.

She asks you to state your query as clearly as you can, ridding it of superfluous content to arrive at a single core question. With the instruction to keep that flowing through your mind, she extends the bowl before you and invites you to look into its depths.

Without touching any part of the bowl or the living light it contains, look through the surface to the picture beneath. Accept the picture that is shown. Do not try to interpret at this time. Accept it and withdraw the focus of your attention. The light dims and the picture fades from sight.

The Oracle places the bowl to one side and lightly touches your third eye in the middle of your forehead. A sharp and piercing sensation is felt, leaving a wake of dizziness and disorientation. Her

action is strange and yet meaningful, a blessing true to her calling. It is as if she invokes her gift within you and shares at a deeper level of awareness.

It is time to leave. Take a few steps backwards before turning aside. Show respect as you make your farewells.

Walk back amongst the trees along the path and let the scene shimmer and fade as you keep in mind the picture given you.

In your own time open your eyes."

Nothing is sure if it is comes from human abilities, and the debate will always rage as to the verity of any other source. Can we ever know the future with certainty? Can we ever know the mind of the Goddess? Yet there is certainty shown from time to time, blinding light of 'knowing' and truth. Interpretation comes clear and unsullied. Here is a philosopher's dream and nightmare.

Legend, Myth and Religious Comparisons

The Jewish Sephirah of Binah I have left in its conventional position [although switching the Pillars], and translates best as 'Understanding'. It also has lesser names as 'Great Sea' or 'Great Mother'.

As an aside, and recalling by way of explanation, Binah is the archetypal womb. It takes the free energy of Force and binds and constricts it within Form. Form, therefore, disciplines Force with a merciless severity. That is the thinking as to why the feminine column has traditionally been dubbed 'the Pillar of Severity', and not a very feminine attribute at all! Certainly in times past, especially the biblical times, the home in any Jewish family would have been ruled by 'Mother'. With that understanding, it becomes much more acceptable to see the traditional placement. However, that is at odds with the present day understanding of the attributes, and that is why I have deliberately placed the Jewish Sephiroth in ways that best fit the usual present day understanding. I follow the pattern used in the placement of the Tarot and Planets.

One insight gained through the Jewish Mystical Tradition is that even at this level of the Great Mother, birth implies death at some time following. Yet death is not a thing to be avoided, but rather embraced, for any kind of death also implies a birth in its own turn, to a different kind of life following on.

A further virtue of Binah is the silence. It is not a 'doing' but a 'being still'. So, the highest feminine aspect of the Divine is expressed as quietness, serenity, an acceptance and understanding of Life and Death, and, by entering the Silence, Divinity is experienced. As the Jewish/Christian scriptures say and infer, "Be still and know that I am God".

I have placed Neptune at this point, although traditionally it is the home of Saturn. Astrologically, Neptune is known as the Mystic, Dreamer or Visionary and these are the qualities I would rather promote through correspondence.

The Tarot card I have chosen is the Hermit. Once again the correspondence with the silence of Binah and the pondering over the mysteries of Life and Death are brought to mind. There is sanctity in withdrawing from the world. There is a holiness that defeats the worldly wise. It epitomizes the Mystic, no matter what gender the hermit is. An Anchoress is just as symbolic as a Hermit, but there is no Anchoress in the Tarot!

I have placed the Dove or the Unicorn here. Both animals have a purity or holiness about them, although one more clearly represents Peace whilst the other Innocence, Magic and Mystery. All correspondences are well within the family grouping.

In the Arthurian legend Morgan fits very well. The Severity or Fey of the Feminine is to the fore. I have no suggestion to make within the Robin Hood legends.

The Oracle is perfect within the Matrix set.

I have deliberately avoided any personalities from the other religions as representing the Goddess, even Mary within the Christian tradition. More thought has been given to the *context* of these traditions, therefore Mary does have a place as she witnesses the death of her son, Demeter grieving for her daughter, Isis searching for the parts of her husband and Ishtar for her lost lover in Hell. Care must be taken not to make too much of a connection and so lose the strength of this position.

Within the Christian tradition I, once again, place a process rather than a person. Whereas the masculine column was championed by Salvation, the way of faith, here Sanctification, the way of grace corresponds. Righteousness is not earned, it is found just to be. Sanctification, or the growth in righteousness, is the quality of God found in a person through grace, not works. It cannot be shown in its own right, but only represented by example of holiness displayed in the saints. Such is the nature of Archetype at this level!

xi. The Rainbow or Temple - Spirituality

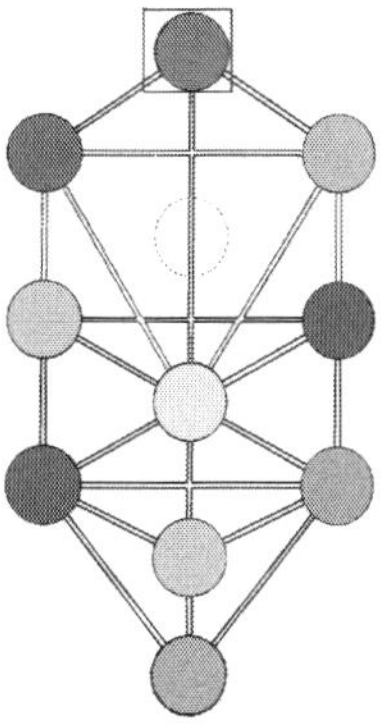

The greatest difficulty of talking about this level of the Qabalah is that we do not have the words necessary to carry out an intelligent or decisive description. Most dialogue of this subject takes place between academic theologians in their ivory towers or between zealous New Agers in their yurts. The ordinary person in the street usually neither cares about nor understands such strange and esoteric concepts. However, to convey the profundity and subtlety of the 'Within' at this level needs such tools, so I am in very real danger of not fulfilling my principles of this overall work.

The original Qabalists saw this position as a description of the Most High and Almighty God. Such a concept is totally beyond human ability to hold, so the end result must forever remain paradoxical, less than satisfactory and the domain of the mystic. The Gnostics, those who immediately followed on from the Jewish Qabalists, also took the same general line, even though they used the system not as means of describing God, but of describing Creation. Their starting point was from a religious persuasion and they proceeded to describe how Creation was manifested into the physical world. The accepted view was that any aspect of Creation, including human kind, starts as an impossible to describe 'spiritual' idea in the mind of God. It then gradually coalesces through the differing levels of being until it eventually establishes itself in the physical world, manifested from spirit, through thought, to the physical. No human mind can even begin to understand the mind of God or

God's awesome power, let alone describe that to other people. It must always be beyond comprehension and conceptualization. That is a religious statement and belief.

My starting point has been from the opposite end of the Qabalah system. It began from the individual's experience of the *bottom* position. It then proceeded as an investigation into the subconscious, gradually venturing deeper and deeper into the less traveled areas of experience, but always understood from the human viewpoint. This was so even when comparing experiences against those generally spoken of as being religious or spiritual in nature. I may have used a Jungian model of the subconscious with its distinct vocabulary, but it has still been an endeavor to be universal and non-partisan, even though I have used my ethnic symbols as preference. With that ground plan held in mind, let me proceed into the rarefied heights, or inner depths, of the home of the Archetype.

Remember from my chapter on symbols, an archetype is the essence of the concept under consideration, but is itself so elusive that it cannot even be processed as a thought until it is concreted within an ethnical context. It lies in the deepest part of the psyche or subconscious and forever slips beyond a conceptual grasp. It is the universal element of that concept that contains the psyche force that can build or destroy the motivating power of that individual's conscious mind. Now, although different words are used, doesn't that sound a bit familiar?

My approach is not a matter of *belief* but *experience*. It is not from a religious persuasion, but is a revelatory process. It does not require a 'party card' strict adherence to a church, cult or religious sect, but an open mind that upholds self-respect and intellectual integrity. It is, however, describing experience that has traditionally been the preserve and domain of the religious, i.e. spirituality in *nonreligious* terms. You do not need to be a Jew, Christian, Atheist or Anything –ist. You need only to ascribe to things in the same way as Jung postulated, with his Archetypes.

I consider that everyone is part spiritual as well as physical and mental, and that to be alive includes a spirituality that is unique as is DNA and fingerprints. There may well be large groupings of experience that are best talked about as spirituality of such and such a religion, but the spiritual walk is a journey for each and every individual. It does not matter what outer religious persuasion or non-persuasion that person may hold, it is still their personal journey. Unfortunately, I also consider that for most people their spirituality is lacking to the point of non-existence - or worse, and this shows in their approach to life, relationship, morals and ethics. It also remains a moot point whether you wish to argue that such an experience is more about relating to the Divine, as an external Being, or relating to the divinity of the individual. There can be no proving it one way or the other.

Whatever you believe it to be, there needs to be a discovery of this position within yourself and a growing awareness of the strength of influence that it can have over *all* aspects of your personality and being. I see it as an experience that holds Authority and a promise of charismatic power over and around you, that cannot be hidden. It invites respect from believers and non-believers alike. It opens the way from potential to actualization.

Self-Awareness

"Close your eyes and once more let the consciousness move from the possible physical points of intrusion to the picture gradually developing in the inner world of the subconscious.

Find yourself in a brilliantly lit and warm cave or grotto, in the middle of which is an altar of black obsidian stone with a dazzling white light upon it. No bowl contains the light this time, but the very light itself is centrally placed upon the altar surface. Veins of gold and silver, with crystal formations running through the rock walls, abound around the grotto. The senses reel with almost an overload of brilliance coming your way. Refracted reds, blues and greens seem to strike you from all directions as the altar light, caught in a crystal facet, flashes spectrums of color around you as you turn or step to one side or the other.

The floor is golden, not only in color but, found by touch and investigation, to be the sacred metal itself. Stand as still as you can for a while and let the awesomeness of that place grow upon you. There is a presence here, here within Mother Earth, but what it is eludes you. It just is. Live in it, acknowledge it, trust it.

On the other side of the altar the golden pathway leads between two almighty columns of crystal rock where, in ages past, the stalagmites and stalactites have joined together. Without touching the altar, make your way around that source of wondrous light and walk slowly between the pillars and along the inviting pathway and revealed tunnel.

In a very short distance the tunnel emerges from a cliff face onto a very deep blue, azure sea. 'Onto' is exactly the phrase to use, for the golden pathway is at sea level and yet traverses the sea as an impossible bridge, making its way towards another shore.

Continue your walk out to sea, but as you follow the way set for you, notice how still the sea is. No rolling swell is observable, although the light is caught a thousand times at any one moment, reflected back in scintillating points from the tiny wavelets on the surface, each hinting at colors caught within the brilliance. At the same time it is if you can almost hear crystal clear notes or tinkling music, created by the light or wavelets. You cross a world of wonder.

All too soon the path nears its destination before an incredibly high sheer rock cliff-face, down which cascades an awesome waterfall. The

path just stops. It finishes before reaching that waterfall, leaving you standing before the heavy spray, surrounded by the finer flowing mist that holds a forever forming, moving and reforming rainbow, as the mist is blown by the draught of the water's own falling.

Open your arms wide to embrace the spectacle. Fill your inner soul with its power of sound and sight. Find yourself literally rising up and flying, following the waterfall to its source, high above the azure sea. There is no sense of fear, no sense of failure, just an anticipation of awe.

As you rise above the cliff edge and the beginnings of the fall, float above the flowing water to a river island just back from the cliff edge. There on the island stands a stone temple, or Stonehenge as it could have been in the minds of its creators. A complete and entire circle of immense stones lies upon upright pillars of great girth, all obsidian black.

The most beautiful rainbow hangs over the island, holding not only the usual seven colors of light, but also other colors, not of this world, on either side of the main arc.

At the center of the Henge is Light. No source is discernable. No form is there to catch the eyes and the mind's understanding. There is just Light.

Despite the overpowering sense of Awe, feel the welcome and invitation held out to you to enter this Temple. Float through one of its portals and fall into the depths of Light, seeing all, but seeing nothing.

After a time the intensity of light begins to dim and you begin to make out the scene that lies before you. The familiarity suddenly makes sense, for you find yourself standing in your secret garden that holds the supported vine. You are in your Garden of Aspiration, looking at the vine that grows there. How you got there is not in question. Just accept the wisdom of the revelation.

After a few moments of reflection, show respect to the vine just as before – is it still the same [?] - and leave your garden in the usual way. Make very sure that the door is shut behind you.

Let that image gently shimmer and fade away. Return to the here and now and in your own time open your eyes."

The visualization contains symbols from many of those that preceded it. Here is Earth, Water, Air and Fire or Light. Here is the grotto of the place of safety from the emotional feminine level or the cave of the Perfect Balance Point. The altar, crystals, pillar, roadway and sea have all been met before, although perhaps not so brilliantly displayed or experienced. The flying is from the bird of the Rational level and the circle of stones from various points of the Qabalah. The whole exercise is an attempt to get as close to the Archetypes as possible, but to the positive light rather than the dark, for both inhabits the soul. The Light is the soul's inner Light, or the Divine itself, that has to be surrendered to in order to experience fully.

It is a journey without end. It is a journey that forever continues. It is a journey that holds immeasurable promise, as the rainbow depicts. It is a discovery that, like an onionskin, there are always more levels or depths to experience. There can be no 'this is my last incarnation' or 'finally arrived' or 'sainthood' whilst incarnate. To even begin to think that reveals such a lack of understanding of maturity and spiritual naivety, that is almost unbelievable. Yet all too often that is the claim of some self-styled guru or leader.

Recalling that one way to avoid the limitations of the simple

Qabalah framework is to include 'hidden' paths and a Qabalah within each of the Sephirah, then to finish by arriving at your starting position seems a logical conclusion and invitation to continue. It encapsulates the entirety of the system and holds every position in tension with the others.

Accept the teaching that you reveal to yourself, and grow.

Therapeutic Involvement and Magical Use

This is the only other position on the Tree of Life where all three uses combine in a single visualization or exercise. There can be no therapeutic or magical use other than knowing the limits of self and awareness of something else that is greater than your sense of self. Yet in the very knowing, there lies the answer to spiritual arrogance and powerlessness. To acknowledge something greater opens both the way to humility and the potential for a greater power to work through you. It is in the surrender that a greater is found. It is only a closed mind that restricts the self.

Legend, Myth and Religious Comparisons

The Jewish Sephirah of Kether and the surrounding space of 'Ain, Ain Soph, Ain Soph Aur' are the highest points of the Jewish Mystical Tradition. As this is not meant to be a treatise on the Jewish understanding let me simplify, being aware that I may be too simplistic.

As soon as a person states that God exists then there is also needed a definition of God, yet a definition limits the object being defined. That is the nature of definition. On the other hand, it is acknowledged that God has no limits so cannot be defined, which is paradoxically included in the definition of God. Therefore God is, yet isn't! God somehow includes all attributes, which is Almighty, but cannot be contained by them. That is the paradox of 'Ain, Ain Soph, Ain Soph Aur'.

Within the paradox is also held the Almighty. Kether, the

Crown, is the highest human attribute awardable. It is the All Knowing, Omnipotent, Ancient of Days, Beyond Understanding God. Note it is pre-Christian, not in chronology, but in understanding or revelation.

I have placed Pluto at this point. Astrologically Pluto is known as the Intensifier, the Unknowable, the Depths and Heights and these must be the qualities of correspondence. It also rules the mysterious House of Crucifixion and Rebirth.

The Tarot card I have chosen is the Fool, not because of any foolishness on my part[!], but because traditionally the Fool is undoubtedly the wisest character of the pack and hides the ways that he works through wit and manipulation. Not necessarily the best description of the Almighty, but one that cynically shows certain attributes of God's ways. He is often depicted as carrying an all-seeing bundle of knowledge but is about to take a step, of faith, off into space! Faith is often mistaken for foolishness.

I have placed the Dragon, Hawk and Eagle at this point. Although the Eagle and Hawk have kingly qualities, it is the Dragon that bests them all by the sheer power conjured up in the name.

Avalon – the Heaven on Earth fits within the Arthurian legend, while Loxley Restored and the desired Peace describe the same within the Robin Hood and Matrix frameworks respectively.

I finish this series with comments upon the Christian tradition and a fear that I will upset more people by doing so. However, one criticism of the Christian church is its appalling arrogance in certain quarters. The scriptural verse "no man comes to the Father except by Me" is sometimes claimed as the justification from Christ himself that spirituality is the monopoly of the church. My position is that although the Jewish Qabalah is pre-Christian in understanding, it presents a truism that is beyond party politics. It shows that even that which is beyond comprehension may be experienced in some way. Therefore, to deny anyone the chance to know God, unless it is in a Christian context, is surely arrogance upon arrogance. The 'knowing' might be limited or very different, but even St Paul, in his letter to the Romans, included such a possibility, and yet he is the one who championed the doctrine of Justification by Faith. Even the Jewish 'unknowable' nature of God at this position is, in fact, touched in a knowing way!

If we hold that the subconscious is whole and the Qabalah is only showing that wholeness in tension with subdivisions, then it is *everyone's* potential experience to explore all parts of the Qabalah and, *by correspondence*, pass not only through the Abyss of Crucifixion, but touch the Crown of Spirituality and embrace the Atonement through the Perfect Balance point. Indeed, "no one comes to the Father but by Me" is upheld, but it is not limited to the church's understanding! It is only limited by a person's blinkered doctrine and spiritual arrogance, not by an Almighty decree. The resulting spirituality may be quite different for different people, but that would be a result of their expectations, their pre-programming, correspondences used within their religious framework - or non-religious framework, etc, etc. It is everyone's privilege to grow. It is the human right.

I rest my case.

7. Conclusion

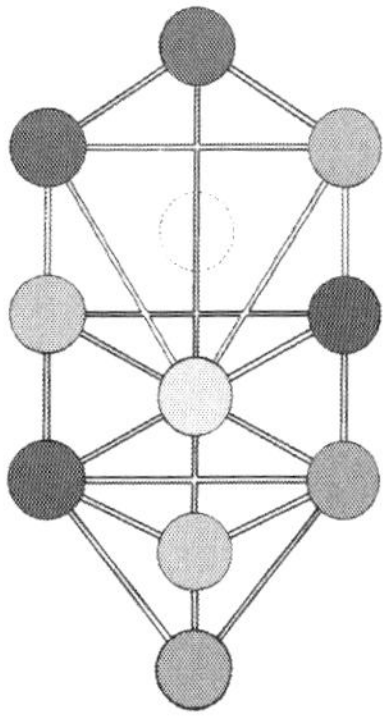

Real life is a series of problem solving. It is meeting challenges or working around them. It is a never-ending struggle that holds dreams, fears, joys and delights in an infinite number and variety of experiences.

Whether we want to or not, we learn from those experiences. That is part of what it means to be human and alive.

Of course, rather than allowing life to arbitrarily lead us along, we often deliberately choose to follow particular experiences in order to learn particular lessons. It is a matter of conscious evaluation and will power that we train and develop certain skills, seek after knowledge and gain understanding, in addition to the seeming arbitrary lessons that come our way.

Every experience is a complex mix of all manner of elements - emotions, conscious thinking, conscious or subconscious memory input, pre-programmed response to situation and stimuli, working within limitations of strength, knowledge, understanding and vision - and so on. It is a matter of careful planning and deliberation to be able to focus on only one aspect of development, but it is never possible to isolate a single aspect of any person's most complex makeup.

What is true of the real physical world is also true of the inner virtual world of the imagination - the subconscious realms. There is a vast wealth of learning possible within the confines of the inner world, never having to lift a physical muscle or venture a foot from our doorstep. Night time dreams or visualizations can make demands or present challenges to the self every bit as real and soul stretching as the real-time physical world.

Just as with the physical world, every visualization or dream can help us to learn about ourselves, and is usually a most complex mix of all that has been said before, but within the confines of the inner world. Everything that happens within, as without, has teaching capacity. However, we can just as carefully plan and execute specific experiences within that inner world to focus on particular lessons, skills or develop understanding of that aspect of life.

The Qabalah is one such system of training and understanding to help develop potential and ability. It is not the only such system that can do this, neither might it be the best system for particular lessons to be learnt, or range of knowledge to be gained, for every single person. People are unique, and sometimes that individuality can only be advanced in ways hitherto not discovered or generally accepted as ways of personal growth and education. In those situations all developed systems, including the Qabalah, cannot be used. The Qabalah is not a panacea of all ills nor meaningful for everyone in every situation. It is not a religion. It is not a brainwashing technique. It is not a cult or Jewish sect.

The Qabalah is a symbol. It is a framework of symbols. It is a framework of exercises, as well as a philosophical understanding at various levels and interests. It is not a framework that will power can be hung upon or simply a system of positive thinking. It is a system that encourages the subconscious to explore itself, and by so doing, invites that self to develop, grow and delight in being truly human and unique. It focuses upon different aspects of the within as far as realistically feasible. It is not something to be taken lightly nor understood as a parlor game. It shows the tensions forever present in every one of us.

It is a wonderful and frightening journey that I invite everyone to try. It is truly the Way of Enchantment.

8. Appendix - Carl Jung on Archetypes

Let me append a few quotes from Jung on his understanding of Archetypes.

"Our personal psychology is just a thin skin; a ripple on the ocean of collective psychology. The powerful factor, the factor that changes our whole life, which changes the surface of our known world, which makes history, is the collective psychology, and collective psychology moves according to laws entirely different from those of our consciousness. The archetypes are the great decisive forces; they bring about the real events, and not our personal reasoning and practical intellect. The archetypal images decide the fate of man."

"In reality we can never legitimately cut loose from our archetypal foundations unless we are prepared to pay the price of a neurosis, any more than we can rid ourselves of our body and its organs without committing suicide."

"We only understand that kind of thinking which is mere equation, from which nothing comes out but what we have put in. That is the working of the intellect. But besides that there is thinking in primordial images, in symbols that are older than the historical man, which are inborn in him from the earliest times, and, eternally living, outlasting all generations, still make up the groundwork of the human psyche. It is only possible to live the fullest life when we are in harmony with these symbols; wisdom is a return to them."

"We must constantly bear in mind that what we mean by 'archetypes' is in itself irrepresentable, but has effects which make visualisations of it possible; namely the archetypal images and ideas. We meet with a similar situation in physics: there the smallest particles are themselves irrepresentable but have effects from the nature of which we can build up a model. The archetypal image, the motif or mythologem, is a construction of this kind."

"The archetype as such is a psychoid factor that belongs, as it were, to the invisible 'ultra-violet' end of the psychic spectrum. It seems to me probable that the real nature of the archetype is not capable of being made conscious, that it is transcendent."

"And these images are not pale shadows, but tremendously powerful psychic factors. The most we may be able to do is misunderstand them, but we can never rob them of their power by denying them."

9. Appendix - Suggested Versions of Qabalah Systems

Each of these systems is only a suggestion. They are not definitive and absolute. Each one must be thought through by every Questor, Therapist or Practitioner and changed to fit with their own inner promptings. There is never only one right and all the rest are wrong. There are only suggested layouts. Some of the layouts or frameworks are not even complete! You need to work on all of them for yourself. Do not automatically accept these ideas as Gospel - they are not, especially in such an ephemeral world as the Within. Try your own variations.

ANIMAL QABALAH

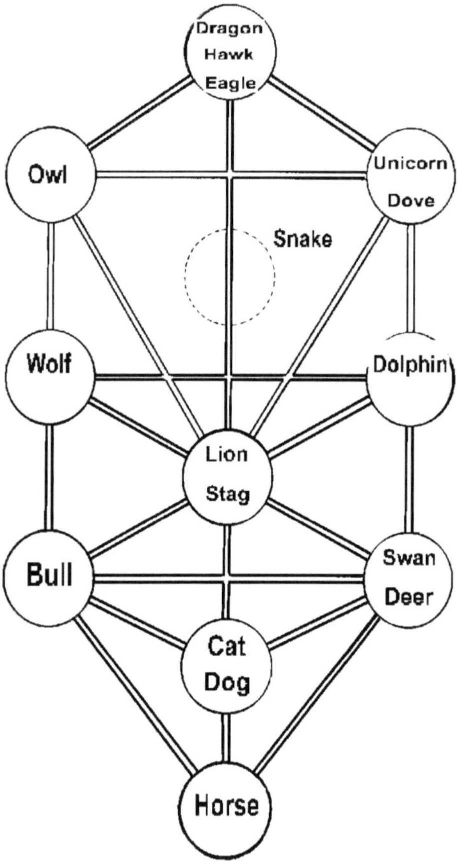

ARTHURIAN QABALAH

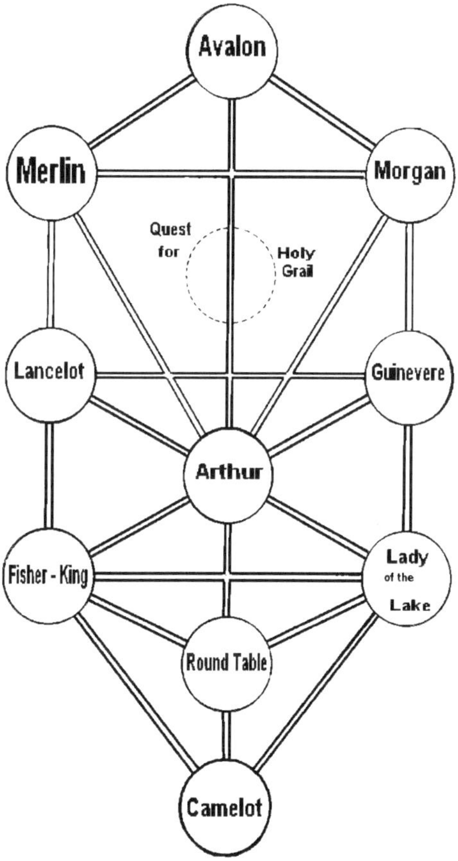

MATRIX QABALAH

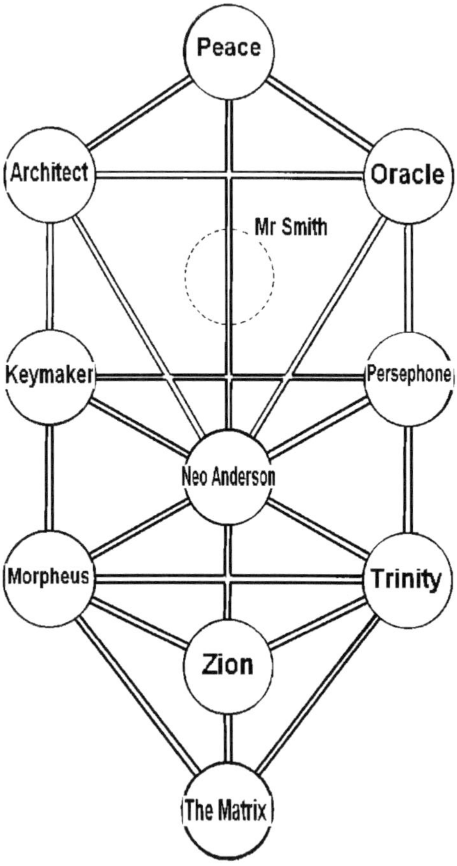

PLANETS QABALAH

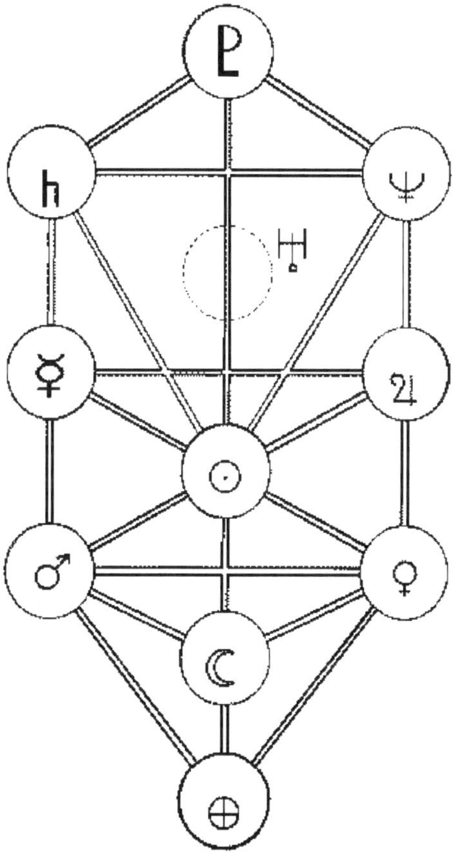

ROBIN HOOD QABALAH

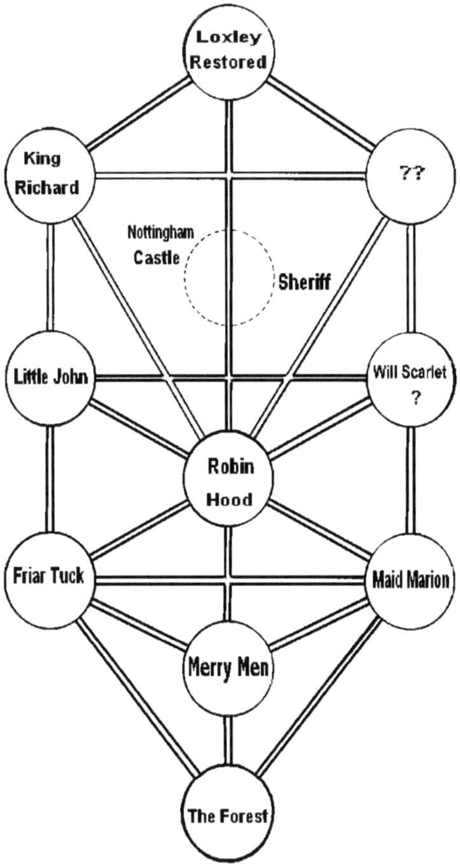

CHRISTIAN QABALAH

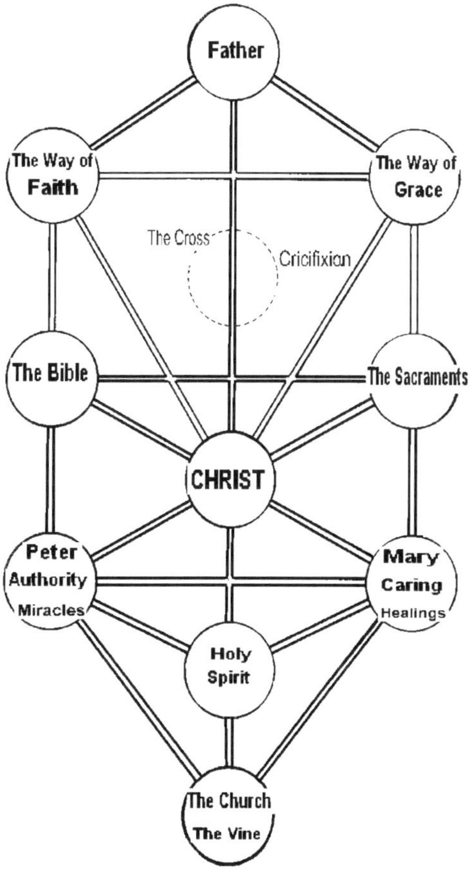

TAROT QABALAH

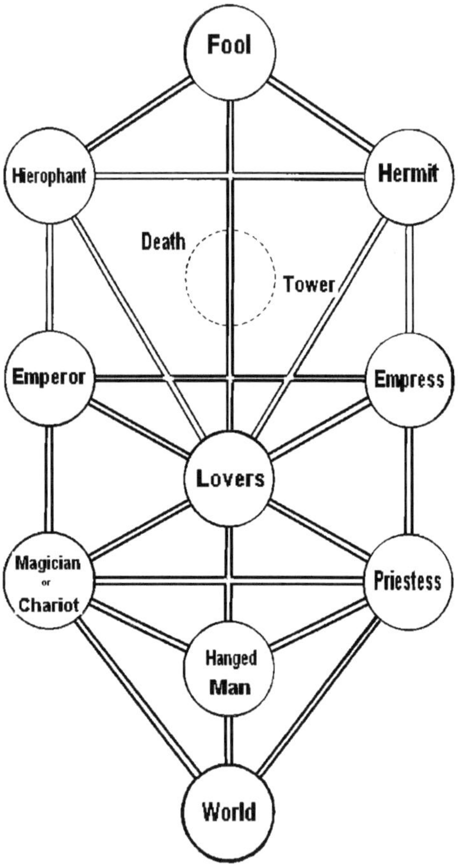

LORD OF THE RINGS QABALAH

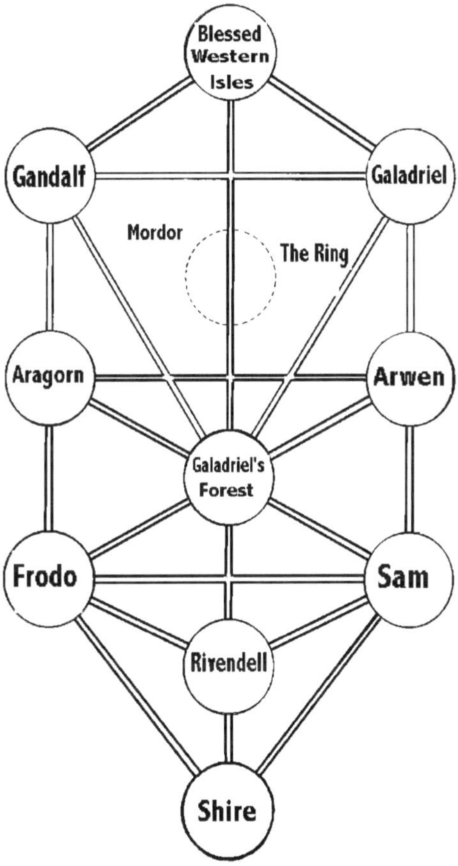

10. Appendix – A Celtic Tree Calendar

Zodiac Sign	Element	Mode	Zodiac Name	Dates	Tree
♈	Fire	Cardinal	Aries	Mar 21 - Apr 20	Holly
♉	Earth	Fixed	Taurus	Apr 21 - May 21	Beech
♊	Air	Mutable	Gemini	May 22 - Jun 21	Chestnuts
♋	Water	Cardinal	Cancer	Jun 22 - Jul 23	Willow
♌	Fire	Fixed	Leo	Jul 24 - Aug 23	Oak
♍	Earth	Mutable	Virgo	Aug 24 - Sep 23	Elm
♎	Air	Cardinal	Libra	Sep 24 - Oct 23	Sycamore
♏	Water	Fixed	Scorpio	Oct 24 - Nov 22	Elder
♐	Fire	Mutable	Sagittarius	Nov 23 - Dec 21	Yew
♑	Earth	Cardinal	Capricorn	Dec 22 - Jan 20	Silver Birch
♒	Air	Fixed	Aquarius	Jan 21 - Feb 19	Rowan
♓	Water	Mutable	Pisces	Feb 20 - Mar 20	Ash

Tree	**Attribute**
Holly	The Initiator's tree. Gets things going. Such a prickly person but a softy inside.
Beech	The steadfast tree. Solid and constant. Person either entrenched or persevering.
Chestnuts	The mercurial tree. Hard working, hard playing. Person just as ready to fight as to nurture.
Willow	The emotional tree. So close to water and tears. Person often needs protection from Life's
knocks.	
Oak	The ruler's tree. Strong and virtuous heart. Person only comfortable when leading.
Elm	The righteous tree. Upright and aspiring.
Person	who perceives great detail but only comfortable with a limited view.
Sycamore	The beautiful tree. Wood can be easily dented. Person who prefers the luxurious lifestyle.
Elder	The healer's tree. Every part has power. Person full of help and understanding but often overlooked.
Yew	The archer's tree. Expansive growth. Person gets to the point, has great enthusiasm but effort is short lived.

Silver Birch	The pioneer's tree. First on the snow line. A person who has great and terrible lessons to learn in Life.
Rowan	The Witches tree. Keeps evil at bay. A person who is strongly individualistic. Clever but may be their worst enemy.
Ash	The magician's tree. The sacred ash grove. The other worldly person who seeks understanding of sacred principles. Often makes things happen.

BOOKS

O books

O is a symbol of the world, of oneness and unity. In different cultures it also means the "eye", symbolizing knowledge and insight, and in Old English it means "place of love or home". O books explores the many paths of understanding which different traditions have developed down the ages, particularly those today that express respect for the planet and all of life.